*Beautiful just!*

LILLIAN BECKWITH

# Beautiful just!

Decorations by Douglas Hall

HUTCHINSON OF LONDON

Hutchinson & Co (Publishers) Ltd
3 Fitzroy Square, London W1

London Melbourne Sydney Auckland
Wellington Johannesburg and agencies
throughout the world

First published 1975
Text and illustrations
© Hutchinson & Co (Publishers) Ltd 1975

Set in Monotype Baskerville
Printed in Great Britain by The Anchor Press Ltd
and bound by Wm Brendon & Son Ltd
both of Tiptree, Essex

ISBN 0 09 125360 8

# Contents

# *Vocabulary*

| | |
|---|---|
| Bodach | Old man |
| Cailleach | Old woman or mother |
| Ceilidh | A meeting for gossip and song |
| Creagach | A rocky place |
| Creagag | The sea wrasse (rock fish) |
| Ha Nyall | No! |
| He breeah | It is fine! |
| He Fluie | It is wet! |
| Oidche Mhath | Good night! |
| Slainte Mhath | Good health! |
| Mho ghaoil | My dear |
| Potach | A cake made from oatmeal mixed with water or, preferably, whisky |
| Strupak | A cup of tea and a bite to eat |
| Sooyan | Young coalfish |
| Souming | The number of animals a crofter is permitted to keep on his croft |

# Fancy Dress

A blend of peat smoke, tobacco smoke and the rhythm of
Gaelic voices drifted languidly through the open doorway
of Janet's cottage where the ceilidh was in progress. It
was early June and all day the land had been spread with
sunshine thick and yellow as Highland cream and even
now, though it was past ten o'clock in the evening, the

9

sun was only thinking of dimming its radiance; the larks were only thinking of moderating their exultation; the cattle on the hills were only thinking of bedding down for the night and the hens were only thinking of returning to their roosts in the henhouse. The Bruachites had just begun their evening relaxation when I joined them.

'Aye, indeed, it's hard when a man has to have one foot on his croft and the other in Glasgow,' Old Murdoch was saying, referring to a crofter from the next village whose funeral the men of Bruach had that day been attending.

'Ach, but he was always such a fast man,' said Morag. 'Flittin' from one thing to another as if he couldn't rest at all.'

'He lived fast an' he died fast,' said Erchy. 'So fast he nearly missed his own damty funeral.'

'How so?' asked Murdoch.

Erchy paused to light a cigarette before replying. 'Why, when we was ready to take him to the burial ground after the minister had finished with him we couldn't find the damty bier to put him on. We searched everywhere an' we was thinkin' we'd have to put the coffin on a wheelbarrow to take it to the grave until Farquhar remembered seein' the bier proppin' up Hamish's haystack last winter.'

'An' that's where it was?' asked Murdoch.

'Aye, right enough, that's where we got it. But by God! it was a good job it was June an' not November or it would have been too dark to bury him by the time we got to the burial ground. He'd have needed to stay out all night.'

There were faint murmurs of condemnation, not of

Hamish's appropriation of the funeral bier for such a mundane purpose but of his neglecting to mention its whereabouts to the gravediggers.

'He was young enough to die,' said Janet in a puzzled tone.

'Aye, an' he must have been sore vexed with himself for dyin' the night before he was to start drawin' his old age pension just,' Morag observed. Her statement was greeted with croons of sympathy.

Murdoch snatched the pipe from his mouth. 'Is that true?' he queried in shocked tones.

Morag nodded emphatically. 'I had it from Fiona at the post office herself,' she asserted. 'Not twelve hours after he died he would have been legible: those were her very words to me.' Morag nodded smugly.

Murdoch, who had been drawing his pension for more than ten years sat back in his chair. 'My, my!' he muttered, and then again, 'My, my!' he said, shaking his head.

'What are you girnin' about, Murdoch?' asked the postman. 'You should put in your new teeths an' then we'd know what you're after sayin'.'

Murdoch spread his lips in a gummy smile. 'My teeths are stayin' where they are now,' he said, indicating the dresser drawer. 'Except for when the minister comes.'

'Ach, come on, Murdoch! Put them in an' let's see how you look in them. What's the use of gettin' new teeths from the dentist an' then leavin' them in the drawer?' The arrival of Murdoch's false teeth had been a minor event in Bruach and there was a chorus of exhortation. 'Come on, Murdoch! Give us a good laugh.'

Janet turned round in her seat and reaching out opened the dresser drawer to take out Murdoch's new dentures. 'They'll not rest now till they see you in them,' she urged jovially. Obediently Murdoch took the teeth, stuffed them into his mouth and bared them in a gorilla-like smile. The company screamed with mirth and Murdoch, himself shaking with laughter, spat the teeth hurriedly into his hand and gave them to Janet who returned them to the drawer.

'There now,' he told them. 'Don't ask to see them again for they're stayin' there till the day I die!'

'And after,' interposed Erchy. 'You won't need teeths where you're goin'. Not to eat hot soup.'

'Oh, here, here.' Murdoch looked a little discomfited by Erchy's remark. Janet hastily brought the subject back to the funeral.

'It would be overwork likely that killed yon fellow so young,' she suggested.

'Ach, the only way yon fellow overworked himself was dodgin' tse income tax mannie,' said Hector, whose acquaintance with income tax assessments was limited to watching them burn. 'Tsat's tse reason for him workin' his croft for six months of tse year an' takin' a job in Glasgow for tse otser six months. He as good as told me so himself.'

'I'm sayin' it was hard all the same,' repeated Murdoch after a short silence. 'A man cannot rightly do two jobs together.'

'Indeed it is so,' agreed Padruig the roadman. 'Don't I know myself what it's like for a man to be needed in two places at one time?'

'An' not to be found in either one of them when the time comes,' taunted Erchy with a wink at the assembled company.

'Why so?' asked Murdoch with pretended surprise and

quickly pushed his pipe between his lips so as to hide a grin.

'Ach, the only times Padruig's usin' his spade these few days past is for plantin' potatoes for his sweetheart Flora,' Erchy elucidated. 'Ever since she's come back to live on the croft she's not wanted for help so long as Padruig's around.'

The return of Flora to her native village after more than thirty years working as a servant on the mainland was the subject of much speculation in Bruach. She was ten years off pension age and she had never previously shown much eagerness to live the crofting life yet here for the past year she had been living and working, apparently contentedly, on the croft she had inherited some years earlier from her parents. There were rumours of a legacy but the Bruachites were sceptical. They knew all Flora's relatives and not one had died leaving more than the amount needed to ship the corpse home for burial and since she had always chosen to be a servant at 'the manse' they dismissed the possibility of her having benefited either by savings or inheritance from such a source. However, it was noticed that she did not stint herself; that there was always a good dram in recompense for work done and so, accepting she had money other than the income from the croft, they could only ponder on its origin.

'Tsat's true what Erchy's sayin',' averred Hector. 'An' I'm tsinkin' we'll be hearin' next she's after gettin' the County Council lorry to take home her peats for her.'

'Here no, surely,' protested Janet.

'The Dear knows my fine Flora's no needin' any County Council lorry,' said Morag. 'She's well able to pay for the hire of her own lorry.' There was a slight trace of envy in her voice.

Padruig leaned forward and lifting a live peat from the fire with his spade-hardened fingers he relit his pipe.

'Sweetheart!' He spoke the word like an epithet. 'There's no harm in givin' a body a hand when it's asked for,' he defended. 'Not when her croft's right there beside the road where I'm workin'.'

'An' you make damty sure that's where you are workin',' Erchy told him. 'But ach, maybe you're wise. I daresay there's a strupak an' a good dram at the end of it.'

Padruig permitted himself a slow, self-satisfied smile. 'Aye, I'm no denyin' it,' he admitted. 'Right enough there's a good dram in it for me most days.' He leaned back puffing at his pipe, savouring their envy.

'Ach, isn't he the wily one?' commented Janet, getting up to swing the boiling kettle half on to the hob.

'Sweetheart or no, I'm after hearin' you took Flora to the Games yesterday, Padruig,' Morag challenged him.

'I did not then,' Padruig repudiated.

'You were sittin' right beside her on the bus,' accused Tearlaich.

'I sat where there was a sit for me,' retorted Padruig, becoming indignant. 'But she paid her own fare. Johnny here will tell you that.' He turned to the bus driver who was sitting on the floor, his back against the wall. 'Is that not the truth of it, Johnny?'

'Aye,' agreed Johnny, 'but not till she'd given up waitin' on you to pay it for her. Ach,' he shook his head, 'You should have seen the look she gave him.'

'I was no seein' it then,' said Padruig loftily.

'Well if she wasn't at the Games with you why is it you were standin' so close together when you were waitin' on the bus to bring you home? I could hardly see you, you were cuddlin' her that close,' Erchy pursued mercilessly.

'Oh, whist, whist!' Padruig replied hastily. 'I got her to stand close to me so the missionary wouldn't get a sight of me. He was passin' at the time an' I didn't want him to know I was at the Games.' There were exclamations of disbelief from the young people.

'Hear tsat now!' scoffed Hector who was lazily netting a coloured glass net float for a pretty young tourist he hoped to seduce the following day. 'Tse man's feared tse missionary will condemn him to hell and burnin' fire because he's been to see a bit of caber tossin' an' listen to a few bagpipes at tse Highland Games.'

The old people, themselves in the thrall of the missionary, were embarrassed by Hector's remark. The young ones risked half suppressed giggles.

'An' what caber tossin'. Why that wee stick they was usin' for a caber would not have made a decent fence stob,' sneered Tearlaich who, like the rest of the Bruach-ites, practised caber tossing with freshly washed-up pit props from the shore having a diameter of about nine inches and weighty with sea water. A man had to be strong indeed to 'toss' such a caber.

'An' the playin' for the bagpipes competition was awful poor, I'm thinkin',' submitted Morag. 'Indeed there was times when I was after puttin' my thumbs into my ears with the noise of them.' She looked about her expecting confirmation. 'It was no so bad for the judge,' she added, 'seein' he was stone deaf anyway.'

Janet handed round mugs of freshly made tea to those who wanted it and before resuming her seat she glanced through the window. 'Here now!' she exclaimed. 'If it isn't Flora herself comin' to ceilidh.'

Flora was small and slight with a long face strained into an expression of unassailable virtue and a mouth that had to be constantly restrained from stretching itself into a smile.

'So here you all are,' she greeted us briskly and while everyone murmured salutations in return we moved along the bench to make room for her to sit down. 'I thought I'd most likely find you here,' she told us.

'Were you wantin' us, then?' asked Murdoch.

'Maybe some of you I want,' replied Flora, taking the cup of tea Janet proffered. 'That's to say those of you that's young enough to be interested in dancin' still.'

'Dancin'?' echoed Tearlaich, who at fifty was reckoned to be among the youngsters of the village.

'Aye.' Flora surveyed their reactions between sips of tea.

'What for would we be goin' dancin'?' asked Padruig, his voice betraying his disappointment. He too was young by Bruach standards but his religion made him almost senile.

'More than that,' continued Flora. 'It's no just a dance but a fancy dress dance I'm speakin' of.'

The old people looked down into their laps but the faces of the young ones brightened with interest.

'What, here in Bruach?' asked the schoolteacher.

'No, indeed,' replied Flora. 'It's over on the mainland in a place where I used to work at the Manse. There's a fancy dress dance goin' to be put on in the hall there an' those of you would like to come then I'm thinkin' of hirin' a bus to take us an' it'll cost you nothin' but the drinkin' money.'

'There's never been that sort of a dance hereabouts, that I've heard of,' mused Erchy. Flora chuckled, a funny throbbing chuckle that made one think it had been too often repressed. 'No, nor will be in my time nor yours, I'm thinkin',' she told him.

'Ach, you'll not get anyone to go from this place,' Tearlaich told her. 'You'll never get folks to dress themselves the way we did at Halloween an' then go off on a bus to some place on the mainland.'

'Indeed no,' responded Flora. 'You'll not be dressin' yourselves up like you did at Halloween. No,' she repeated when Tearlaich looked at her in surprise. 'You'll need to come in somethin' better than old clothes you've taken from out of your lofts.' She turned to me. 'You'll know about fancy dress, Miss Peckwitt,' she said and looked at me questioningly.

'It's a long time since I was at a fancy dress dance,' I told her.

'No matter,' she replied. 'You can tell them some ideas about what to wear.' She looked at the young schoolteacher. 'What about you, Elspeth? You must have seen fancy dress dances when you were at college, did you not?'

'Aye,' admitted Elspeth. 'I went to one once as Mary, Queen of Scots,' she confessed.

'Right enough then,' said Flora. 'An' what about Jeannac here goin' as Meg Merrilees?'

'Is that the idea of it?' said Tearlaich as enlightenment dawned. 'You dress up as somebody you learned about at school?'

'You can go as anything,' the schoolteacher started to explain. 'You can put on a pair of horns an' go as a stag.'

'One of you could dress up as a policeman, or even as a minister,' I suggested daringly but except for Flora who flashed me a conspiratorial smile the rest ignored my suggestions and the conversation continued as various proposals as to suitable attire were put forward.

'Erchy should go dressed up as a bottle of whisky,' suggested Johnny.

'Here no! They'd have me buried alive the minute they saw me,' said Erchy, referring to the Bruach custom of burying their whisky bottles outside the dance hall.

'What I'm wantin' to know is why you yourself is so keen to go to the dance that you'll be wantin' to hire a bus?' Old Murdoch said.

Flora put down her cup. 'Well now, I'll tell you for why,' she began and while we all listened avidly she told us the story of how she had come by her 'legacy' and why she particularly wanted to go to the fancy dress dance.

'As you know,' she began, 'I've been workin' the past three years for a Free Presbyterian Minister an' then one day after a telegram comes for him he calls me into his study. The man was in a terrible state! I knew that when the first thing he did was ask me to sit down. Then he says, "How long have you been with us now, Flora?" "Three years, near enough," says I. "An' have you been content with us?" says he. Well, I told him I'd been content enough though the Dear knows workin' for that old fright of a wife he has I used to think sometimes I would be better off workin' in a salt mine. Anyway the next thing is he's tellin' me I'll have to leave. It fairly took my breath away at first an' I was just goin' to tell him I was thinkin' of doin' that anyway when he shows me this telegram.' Flora paused to ensure she had our complete attention. 'I don't like telegrams but I knew I had no relations that could have passed on to give me a shock so I just stares at him. Then he tells me of how he was travellin' on the train one day an' not havin' his bible with him at the time, so he says,' she grimaced knowingly, 'he picks up this paper that someone's left behind an' when he'd read all that was fit to read he started to do the competition an' when he'd done it he was feelin' that pleased with himself he decided to send it off. It wasn't until he came to address the envelope that he noticed he'd been readin' a Sunday newspaper!'

The Bruachites were aghast. A 'Wee Free' minister reading a Sunday paper was such an unthinkably wicked thing to do they were as agog to hear the rest of Flora's tale as they would have been to hear the final denouement in a detective story.

' "Well, Flora," says he, an' this is his story. "It somehow got posted along with some other letters I was postin' at the same time an' now has come this telegram today to say I've won first prize." ' No one spoke and Flora continued, 'I could see he was in a right mess with the Church Assembly no doubt wantin' him thrown out of the Church an' his wife no doubt wantin' him thrown into the sea but what I couldn't see was how it had to do with me. Then he points out that not only have we the same surname, himself an' me, but we have the same initial too. "You're Flora an' I'm Farquhar," says he. "So Flora," he begs me, "if you will say it was yourself won the competition an' have your name go in the papers then you're welcome to every penny the devil has tried to tempt me with." '

'An' you took it?' asked Morag with faint disapproval.

'I did indeed,' replied Flora. 'It was worth gettin' acquainted with the devil for it to my way of thinkin'.'

'But you had to leave your place through it?' asked Murdoch.

'Aye, indeed,' replied Flora. 'A Godly man like him

couldn't go on having a sinner like me that did competitions in Sunday newspapers livin' under the same roof as himself now, could he? Not once my name got into the paper?'

'An' were you no sorry at all to leave?'

'Not a bitty,' asserted Flora. 'I was kind of fancyin' comin' back to the croft anyway. Ach, the minister himself wasn't so bad but his wife was such an old fright the poor man would hardly dare to look at a flower in his garden on the Sabbath. I'm tellin' you without a word of a lie she was that mad with religion she used to go sniffin' round the house in case I'd been wicked enough to bring in a bit of scented soap to wash myself with.'

I found myself wondering why Flora should have chosen to work at a 'Wee Free' manse and had I not been aware of the old people's indoctrination of their children with the idea that if they went away to be servants they must go either to the manse or to the laird's house I would have suspected she had a masochistic streak in her.

'In a way I'm after seein' now why you're so keen to get to this fancy dress dance,' said Tearlaich. 'But neither the minister nor his wife is goin' to be seen anywhere near that, surely?'

Flora let out a ripple of laughter. 'No, what I'm hopin' is there'll be a photographer there from the paper so that maybe I'll get my picture in it for the minister to see. I know the mannie that does the pictures,' she added, 'an' I believe when I tell him what I want he'll be well pleased to do it for me.'

'Why, what will you be dressin' yourself up as, then?' asked Erchy.

Flora treated him to a brazen smile. 'I'm goin' to dress myself up as one of these nuns,' she told him, 'an' I'm goin' to be carryin' a big bundle of Sunday papers under my arm.' She stood up and while dusting some crumbs of scone from her skirt enjoyed the varying expressions of amusement, admiration and disapproval. 'Think about what I've been sayin' now an' make up your minds in good time,' she instructed them. 'You'll have a good time, I promise you that.' She winked at them.

'I can tell you right now,' said Erchy. 'I'm damty sure I will come so long as somebody promises to see me safely home again afterwards.'

'Didn't I tell you I'm hirin' a bus,' she reminded him.

'Ach, no, but what I'm meanin' by safe is nothin' to do with the bus. See now,' he explained, 'when I'm at a dance I'm likely to take a good drink an' it's then the women get at me.' The 'women' hooted with laughter.

'I'll promise to protect you from the women,' Flora assured him.

'Hell!' parried Erchy ungratefully. 'Who will be protectin' me from you then?'

'Away with you, man,' Flora teased. 'I've not worked for ministers all these years without learnin' to keep myself to myself.' She opened the door. 'It's a grand night,' she called as she stepped out into the still golden twilight. 'Oidche Mhath!'

'Oidche Mhath!' we called after her.

I started to laugh. 'Flora's certainly given you all plenty to think about, hasn't she?' I said. 'And this fancy dress dance sounds as if it might be a lot of fun.'

'I wouldn't mind goin' myself,' said Johnny. 'That's if Miss Peckwitt here will fix up somethin' for me to wear.'

'I'll do that,' I promised.

'An' what about me?' joked Murdoch. 'Will you no

find somethin' for me to dress up as so that I can go?' He wheezed with laughter.

Erchy grunted. 'You, you old bodach! Why if you're thinkin' of goin' Miss Peckwitt will no be needin' to find somethin' for you to dress yourself up in. All you will need to do is put in your new teeths an' go as a horse.'

# Urgent Ernest

'Ach! I'm as tired as an old horse,' declared Morag as I
drew near. She had been collecting driftwood along the
shore and the roped bundle lay beside her while she
rested before carrying it up the brae. Nearby Hector and
Erchy were painting and patching their boats in prepara-
tion for the coming season and since it was the spring

holiday a troop of barefoot children skipped nimbly from rock to rock, pelting one another with crabs and limpet shells and brandishing stems of 'staff' from which every now and then they bit large chewy mouthfuls. Unlike town children who seem unable to enjoy themselves without the accompaniment of discordant yelling Bruach children were astonishingly quiet in their play. They teased as much, taunted, chaffed and goaded as much, as their town counterparts, yet their undulating Gaelic voices were no more intrusive than bird song. Even when missiles found their targets or when feet slipped on wet rocks their protests were muted; only small explosions of laughter occasionally broke the bounds of their restraint.

I dropped my sack on the shingle beside Morag and sat down.

'I'm thinkin' what you have there makes a softer seat than driftwood,' she observed, indicating my sack. I nodded. There had been several drums of kapok washed up on the shore and the men of the village had chopped open some of them so those of us who fancied making cushions or eiderdowns from the kapok could take along our sacks and fill them. Of course officially the drums were the property of the Receiver of Wrecks but Bruach had its own strict code of practice so far as flotsam and jetsam were concerned. Bodies and explosives were reported to the police; useful items were finder's property while those of no use but likely to bring in salvage money were notified to the 'Customs mannie'; the rest was left to come and go as it pleased. The kapok was about a mile away along the shore from Bruach but since a sack stuffed tight full made only a light burden the necessary journey to collect it was a pleasure rather than a chore.

'Behag was after gettin' herself some of it yesterday,' Morag informed me.

'I know,' I admitted. 'I met her there. I got a sackful yesterday too. And another one the day before,' I added.

'Whatever will you be wantin' with all that?' asked Morag. 'I thought you were sayin' you needed enough for a cushion or two just.'

I smiled ruefully. It was true that I needed and had intended to get only enough kapok for a few cushions but life in Bruach was making me acquisitive: the constant frustrations one encountered when trying to obtain the things one needed at the time one needed them was responsible for my hoarding a variety of articles which I was unlikely to have any use for but since I hated to see anything going to waste whether it was a trawl bobbin or a tin of shaving cream my pile of treasures from the shore continued to mount steadily over the years until it threatened to take up as much space on my croft as did my henhouse. And now, here I was carrying home my third sack of kapok when already I had amassed many times the quantity needed to stuff a few cushions and since kapok requires to be stored in a dry place and the dry places in and around my home were already packed to capacity with far more vital supplies than cushion filling Morag's question made me suspect, not for the first time, that perhaps my acquisitiveness was becoming something of an obsession.

'Oh well,' I said defensively, 'it's a grand day for beach-combing.' It was indeed a grand day, not just for beach-combing but for sitting and staring and listening and chatting in the warm sunshine. The sky was veined with thin cloud like the grain in old wood; the sea was netted with silver; the tide rustled among the rocks, and a low, seeking wind harried shreds of dry seaweed along the shingle.

'You would think there must be plenty of fish out there,' observed Morag, her eyes on a turmoil of gulls which was concentrated on a patch of sea about half way between Bruach and the island of Rhuna. She turned and called to the men at their boats. 'The gulls is findin' fish, I doubt.'

Erchy and Hector looked up and screening their eyes against the sun focussed their attention on the birds. 'Aye, it's sooyan, likely,' Erchy called back. Glad of the flimsiest excuse to stop work Hector sprackled over to sit on the shingle beside us.

'I think if some of these scientist fellows would watch the gulls an' find out more about them they wouldn't be needin' to invent all these machines they have for findin' the fish,' said Morag. 'They would need just to train the gulls to find it for them.'

'Aye,' agreed Hector. 'Tse gulls would find tse fish all right but would folks want to eat tse sort of fish tse gulls found?' He screwed his face into an expression of distaste. 'I mind seein' gulls eatin' some mighty queer fish at times.'

Erchy came over to join us. 'I've not seen so much of you since you were back from your tour,' he told Morag.

'Indeed an' that's true,' returned Morag. 'I'm that tired since I was back I believe I could sleep on a plank on edge. That's what my tour has done for me.'

Morag had recently spent three weeks' holiday visiting various relatives in and around Glasgow and having returned to plunge immediately into the spring work on the croft neither she nor anyone else had found much time for ceilidhing.

'I'm hearin' you enjoyed yourself, then.' Erchy's voice

sounded almost accusing, justifiably perhaps since Morag was in the habit of disparaging not only Glasgow but most of its inhabitants.

'I enjoyed myself fine but for the last week of it I was in Glasgow. I believe it was that took the strength out of me. It's a gey fast city,' she added disapprovingly.

'It's fast right enough,' agreed Hector. 'When I was tsere lookin' for a boat I seen tse folks rushin' at everytsin' like hens to a feedin' bowl; tsen as soon as tsey were in tsey were wantin' out an' pushin' one another tse same as sheep through a gap when tsey has a dog at tsem. I used to stand an' watch tsem just tryin' to make sense of it all.'

'Aye well,' rejoined Erchy, 'there's one thing nobody will ever see you do an' that's rush.'

Hector smiled blandly. 'No indeed,' he replied. 'Why would I rush when tsere's plenty to do tsat for me?'

'An' the drinkin'!' Morag resumed, cutting short their chaff. 'The drinkin' was terrible just! I've never seen the like.' I slid a glance at Erchy who, given the opportunity, could himself give an impressive drinking performance but he affected not to notice and continued staring at the feeding gulls. 'An' not just the men,' Morag went on, her tone growing more sanctimonious. 'I was invited to take tea with a swanky friend of Ina's at three in the afternoon an' when we got there didn't the woman bring out a bottle of whisky an' pour out a dram for each of us?' She turned to me. 'Whisky!' she repeated. 'For a woman, at three o'clock in the afternoon. Can you believe that now?'

I hoped my expression was suitably scandalized. 'Did you refuse it?' I asked.

'Indeed I did not then, seein' it was set out for me I

couldn't very well not drink it for fear of offendin' the woman,' she countered virtuously.

'Whereabouts did you go when you were away then?' Erchy asked.

'All kinds of places,' said Morag. 'We went to what they called a ceilidh but the singin' was on the stage mostly.'

'Were they good singers?' asked Hector.

'Oh, right enough some of them were good,' she conceded with some reluctance. 'But I believe I've heard better here in Bruach.' Morag secretly believed that Bruach was bursting with every sort of skill and talent. She paused. 'An' they had a fiddler there on the stage that was so long sharpenin' his strings before he would start to play I was thinkin' he'd wear through them first.'

We were interrupted by one of the children who came skipping over the shingle calling and beckoning. 'Are you wantin' to see a killer?' he asked, looking directly at me. 'He's right inshore there.' I leapt up and clambering on to a rock was in time to see the bulk of a rounded body and a long sword-like fin disappearing beneath the water but though I continued watching for some minutes the whale did not break surface again and I returned to my companions.

Accustomed to such sights they had not bothered to stir from where they sat. 'It was huge!' I told them excitedly. 'Honestly, I'd say the fin was six foot high above the water.'

'Aye.' Erchy's tone was indulgent. 'It would be a bull likely.'

I continued to gaze fascinatedly at the sea. 'What strange creatures there could be down there without our ever having seen them,' I mused.

'Maybe a mermaid or two,' suggested Erchy with a faint smile.

'If there was mermaids there surely Hector here wouldn't be for stayin' on the shore,' said Morag.

'No, nor me,' Erchy was quick to add. 'I would be out there with a net soon enough.'

'And what would you do supposing you caught a mermaid?' I asked.

'I wouldn't be tellin' you,' he replied flippantly.

'No, seriously,' I persisted. 'Supposing one day you did actually catch a mermaid in the net and haul it aboard your boat what would you do with it?' Erchy looked self-conscious.

'We'd make our fortunes out of it, tsat's what we'd do wis it,' said Hector. 'We'd have all tse papers an' tse fillums payin' us good money just to get a look at it.'

Erchy drew up his knees and hugged them. His expression had become thoughtful. 'No, I would not then,' he said. 'If I was to get a mermaid in the net then I would put her back in the sea again.'

'Never!' protested Morag.

'Aye,' insisted Erchy.

'You would surely try an' get hold of a camera an' take a picture of her first?' challenged Morag.

'I don't believe I would do even that,' asserted Erchy.

We all looked at him but he ignored us and continued to stare reflectively at the sea.

'Why?' I asked him.

'Ach, mermaids is mermaids an' people is people,' he said evasively but I repeated my question. He shifted uneasily. 'The way I see it then is if I was to get a mermaid in the net I'm damty sure she would be scared enough without a lot of strangers after excitin' themselves over her. An' if the papers an' the fillums got to know of it she would get not a moment's peace from then till the day she died.'

'But, man, it is you would get tse money,' expostulated Hector. 'You would be a millionaire likely.'

'I wouldn't care about that,' said Erchy. 'I wouldn't even take a camera to her unless I could make the picture without anyone else seein' it.'

'You would make plenty of money from a picture of her just,' Morag assured him.

'Aye, an' wouldn't a picture of her bring every boat in the country here with nets searchin' for her?' Erchy demanded. 'No,' he repeated, 'the day I catch a mermaid will be the day I throw a fortune back into the sea an' there's no one but myself will be the wiser.'

'The Dear help you then,' murmured Morag. I slanted her a wry smile and recalling how these same Highlanders had once scorned the fortune offered by the English for the capture of Bonnie Prince Charlie I suspected that faced with the problem her reaction would be the same as Erchy's.

It was decidedly pleasant sitting and chatting in the sunshine but I had much to do at home so picking up my sack I made a move to go. Morag struggled to her feet, intimating that she too must be on her way. I had gone only a few paces when Erchy called after me. 'You must have more than enough of that stuff!' He nodded at my sack. I confessed I had. 'I don't know why you bother with it at all then when there's plenty other things you could be gatherin' on the shore an' maybe earnin' yourself good money doin' it,' he informed me.

'What sort of things?' I asked sceptically. From time to time I had heard stories of lucrative finds on the shore some of which stories I suspected to be wildly exaggerated but I had never been lucky enough to come across anything that could be considered of even scant market value.

'Net floats,' Erchy replied. 'There's a fellow in the fishin' paper sayin' there's a shortage of net floats an' he's willin' to buy secondhand ones for good money so long as they're sound.'

'Glass floats?' I asked, still unimpressed. I had been collecting coloured glass net floats from the shore ever since I had come to live in Bruach and they were among my most cherished trophies. I was certainly not interested in selling them to anyone.

'No, but the aluminium ones,' Erchy explained.

'Honestly?' There was always an abundance of aluminium net floats washed up during the storms and apart from splitting them to make rather unstable feeding bowls they were of little use. One either left them on the shore to be taken away by the next high tide or, if one was feeling sportive, one threw them back into the sea. It sounded too good to be true that a time had now come when one could actually sell them for money.

'Aye, true as I'm here,' asserted Erchy. 'I'll bring you the paper with the advertisement in it. You will get the name of the man for yourself.'

A few days later, returning from milking the cow, I found the promised paper on the table. As I slipped off my jacket my startled eye lit on a banner headline across the front page. 'Writ Nailed to Purser' it read. I dropped my jacket on a chair and picking up the paper was relieved to discover that the victim of the impaling was not a human being but a type of boat described as a 'Purse-net Seiner', esoterically referred to as a 'Purser'. I settled down with a cup of coffee and the fishing paper and soon found myself chuckling over other intriguing headlines. 'Skipper Buried' stated one baldly and I found myself wondering how skippers were usually disposed of that the burial of one should merit a headline. Then there was 'Firemen Hose Down Skipper!' which reported an incident at a certain port where the amateur fire fighters holding their very first practice drill had, due to a complexity of instructions, unintentionally directed their hose on to a trawler which had just moored alongside the pier. As the wheelhouse door opened the skipper had emerged to be met by a sudden jet of water which had knocked him sprawling on the deck. The paper gave only the bare facts of the incident but visualizing the scene and being aware of the shortness of temper attributed to most trawler skippers I could imagine that in this particular instance water, so far from quenching, would more likely have fuelled a roaring fire of invective.

When I had browsed over the headlines I quickly scanned the text which was of little interest to the uninitiated except for a delightful sentence which I copied down in my notebook:

'Forty fish filleters from Fraserburgh spent their Fair Fortnight visiting freezer factories . . .'

If only the freezer factories had been in Frankfurt, I thought, the sentence would have provided a tongue twister to rival 'Peter Piper'. Reminding myself that I had been loaned the paper for a more serious purpose I turned to the advertisements and eventually found the address of the man who was prepared to buy washed-up net floats. So for a few weeks I was able to feel virtuous in combining the pleasure of roaming the shore with the serious business of collecting net floats. When I had

amassed a suitable quantity I prevailed upon the postman
to provide me with a mailbag in which I could send them
away. There seemed to be an unlimited supply of unused
mailbags in Bruach and though officially I supposed they
were classed as damaged or soiled most of them were in
fact in perfect condition. They were used for carrying hay
to the cattle; they were opened out and used as covers for
haycocks or as cloaks for humans. I had even dyed one
and made myself a very efficient windcheater out of it.
The postman obligingly turned up the next day with a
mailbag and my floats were duly despatched via the
carrier. A few weeks later I was delighted to receive a
money order. So I collected more floats, begged another
mailbag and sent off a second consignment. It was six
weeks this time before I heard anything and then it was
not the postman bringing the expected money order but
the carrier who deposited an entirely unexpected bundle
outside my gate. Since I had not ordered any goods to
arrive via the carrier I naturally assumed he had made a
mistake but examining the label I saw that the bundle
was from the float buyer and that there could be no
mistake about its being addressed to me. On investigation
I was puzzled to find that the bundle contained a piece
of herring net and a length of creel rope and since neither
were of any use to me I was certain that the float buyer
had made a mistake when addressing the label. Undoubtedly it should have been sent to one of the fishermen
of Bruach so I asked Erchy if he knew of anyone who had
ordered net and rope.

'Oh, did no one tell you?' he began adroitly. 'Yon
fellow is after sendin' us goods now instead of money for
our floats. We reckon we get a better deal this way than
if we take the money.'

'I see,' I said. 'And when you were making this barter arrangement no one thought to leave me out of it?'

Erchy had the grace to look slightly discomfited. He bent down to inspect the net. 'See now, that would cost you a pound or two if you were to buy it. So would the rope. More than you would get for the floats supposin' it was money he was after payin' you for them,' he complimented me.

Perceiving that willy-nilly I had been co-opted into providing Erchy and his confederates with replacement fishing gear I still played out the role of the unsuspecting novice.

'What do I want with all that creel rope?' I demanded.

'You could use it as clothes rope,' he suggested.

I laughed ironically. There was enough rope to stretch almost from one end of the village to the other. 'I doubt if I'll live long enough to use all that up,' I said. 'And as for the net,' I shrugged my shoulders, 'What use have I for a herring net?'

'Ach, you'll likely find a use for it,' he comforted. Because Erchy had seen me make leftover food into tasty dishes and make old dresses into new cushion covers he seemed to have a touching faith in my ability to produce a masterpiece out of something as uninspiring as a piece of herring net. 'You could do well out of it, I'm thinkin',' he added.

'How?' I asked.

'Well, there's Hector,' he suggested. 'Isn't Hector always havin' to borrow a net whenever he goes to the fishin'?'

'Hector always has to borrow something whenever he does anything,' I retorted. I knew Hector too well to have any illusions about his ever recompensing me for the

34

net except perhaps by occasional gifts of illicit fish. I had
not known then, however, that in Bruach when a single
woman or a widow owns a net which is borrowed for the
fishing that woman is entitled to a share of the catch and
there came a day when, my net having been borrowed and
the herring having obligingly swum into it, I found myself
the recipient of a whole creelful of fresh fish. For hours I
scaled and gutted and salted. I ate the herring fresh; I
made it into paste; I boiled it and mixed it with the
poultry mash and when it started to smell I dug it as
manure into the garden.

'Didn't I tell you you would do well out of your net?'
asked Erchy whose eyes were glowing with the excitement of 'herring fever'.

'You certainly did,' I replied, belching discreetly.
Herring invariably gave me indigestion.

I ceased collecting net floats and reverted to my
former practice of heaving them back into the sea whenever I found them but a month or so later the carrier
delivered another bundle from the float buyer and the
same evening the postman brought me a postcard
scrawled in green ink and with almost every other word
accorded the dignity of a capital letter.

'I am Happy sending Goods,' it read. 'Many net floats
Wanted Urgent Ernest.'

I debated whether or not to return the bundle unopened
to 'Urgent Ernest' but since doing so would have involved
me in freight charges and since he had been trusting
enough to send me goods without waiting for a consignment of floats I decided that the sensible thing to do was
to collect more net floats and send off another mailbag-
ful in return. This consignment brought me a letter
which, like the postcard, was scrawled in bright green ink

and liberally sprinkled with capitals, the only punctuation being exclamation marks.

'Dear Friend', it began
'Are you in Need of Spare Parts! I have at the Back of The Store Ernest! socked in Oil and Swearing as Good as New! Hundreds of Different! No rust on Ernest! Will send soonest if you are Missing! I am Eighty and still need many more Floats Urgent! . . . Your friend in the Lord!'

The letter itself I thought was worth another sackful of floats and I resumed my quest though admittedly with less enthusiasm than when I had expected to be paid in cash for my efforts. Since I did not consider myself in need of spare parts and since, to be honest, I was a little apprehensive of what the postman or the carrier might bring if I admitted to any deficiency I did not reply to the letter from my 'Friend in the Lord!' but despite this there arrived for me a small sack containing a miscellany of large bolts and nuts and washers; a single rowlock that would fit no boat in Bruach and a mysteriously shaped metal object which was expertly identified for me by Hector as 'A tsing for doin' somesin' wiss.' All the contents of the sack, as had been so 'ernestly' claimed, were well soaked in oil as I found to my dismay when I emptied them out on to the kitchen floor. I bestowed them on Erchy who seemed pleased enough to get them and resolved that from that day forward I would send no more net floats. But I had reckoned without the old float buyer. At varying intervals bundles and parcels continued to arrive inexorably and urged on by quaint green-inked exhortations I began to liken myself to the Sorcerer's apprentice so compelled did I feel to gather more and more net floats in order to satisfy my 'Friend in the Lord!'

It was with mingled relief and regret that eventually I received a green-inked letter telling me that the shortage of net floats was over and thanking me most 'Ernestly!' for my help. It was not long afterwards that Erchy brought the news that the old net float buyer had 'passed on'.

'I should like to have met him,' I said. 'He must have been a real character if his letters are anything to go by.'

'Aye, right enough I believe he was that,' said Erchy. 'They're sayin' he hadn't much in the way of schoolin' but he wasn't wantin' sense when it came to the business.'

'He sounded a very religious man,' I said.

'Not just religious,' corrected Erchy. 'But he was good with his religion. Not like some. They say he treated the fellows that worked for him well too,' he added.

'It's nice to hear that,' I murmured, but as I thought of Ernest! socked in oil at the Back of the Store! I wondered.

# The Whelk Gathering

'Come the first calm day of the tide an' I swear I'll not wait even to put the pot on the fire before I'm away to the whelks,'* declared Peggy Ruag with mock exasperation.

'Indeed then it's the men will be swearin' when they'll

* Whelks are known as winkles on the English market.

be after comin' back to find there's no potatoes for their dinner,' warned the prim-mouthed Kirsty.

'No matter,' supported Anna Vic. 'Didn't I tell our own Lachy the other day just he can cook his potatoes himself as soon as a good day comes for the whelks.' She ended with a giggle of bravado.

Fiona and Peggy Ruag exchanged furtive smiles, knowing well that 'our Lachy' ensured his mother's constant ministrations by affecting complete indifference to hunger. If she was not there to cook a meal for him Lachy would simply go without food which so worried his soft-hearted mother that no matter how demanding were her other chores she somehow contrived to have a cooked meal ready for her son when he came in.

'Ach, but this weather's a curse right enough,' grumbled Peggy Ruag lightly.

Fiona and the three women had been on their way home from milking their cows when a savage squall of hail had sent them hurrying for the shelter of the Creagach.

'I'm hearin' there's a good price on the whelks this year,' said Anna Vic, taking off her headscarf to shake it free from hailstones.

'Indeed, I'm hearin' that too,' agreed Kirsty, rubbing at her stiff, red hands.

'You'll be comin' to the whelks yourself now that you've left school, Fiona?' Peggy Ruag asked.

'Ach, I might just as well,' replied Fiona noncommittally.

'Me, I'm just strainin' to get at them an' I don't mind tellin' you,' confessed Peggy Ruag who though half Highland had not one whit of the Highlander's innate reserve. She chuckled. 'It's this new catalogue that's makin' me so keen to get started,' she explained. 'There's that much in it I want I could do with the whelks being in season all the year round.'

'Here, no, don't say that,' protested Kirsty. 'If there was whelks in the spring an' summer when would we see our beds for the work that would be in it?'

'We'd fall asleep in the hay surely, an' get ourselves stacked along with it!' Anna Vic's shrill schoolgirl laughter made her fat stomach quake like a bog.

The whelking season lasted from November to March, conveniently filling the period between harvest and sowing and on relatively calm days when the ebb tide occurred during the hours of daylight the islanders, trussed with extra clothes almost to the point of im-mobility would converge on the shore with pails and sacks ready to begin the whelk gathering.

Fiona, who had left school only that summer, was as eager as Peggy Ruag for the weather to improve so that she could go whelk gathering and like Peggy it was the arrival of the new mail order catalogue that was respon-sible for her eagerness. Ever since she had been old enough to carry a pail she had shared increasingly in the work of the croft, helping to harvest the potatoes and turnips; gather in the hay and corn; gut and salt the herring for winter food and carry home creels of peat for the fire, but such work was instinctive; its reward the comfort and well-being of man and beast. But the rewards of whelking were cheques from the buyer at Billingsgate; cheques which old Marie at the post office would cash and with cash, as Peggy Beag had said, you could buy things from the catalogue – glamorous things like the new coat Fiona had set her heart on. 'Janette', the caption read, 'an enchanting coat in smooth blue wool mixture with a sumptuous collar of squirrel coney.' Fiona had never in her life possessed a shop coat, her mother having made all her coats from the lengths of rough hairy tweed her Aunt Sarah wove. But now she had left school she had the opportunity to go whelk gathering and she planned to earn enough money during the season to buy 'Janette'.

'Aye, well, I believe that's the squall over for a whiley,' said Anna Vic and the women moved from the shelter of the Creagach to stand for a minute gazing at the thundering walls of green water that were smashing themselves into a filigree of foam against the rocks of the shore.

'It's no lookin' like good whelkin' weather at all,' observed Anna Vic sadly.

But during the night the wind was tamed to a shifty grumbling which by morning had subsided to a steady raw breeze that crisped the short grass of the crofts with frost. Fiona rose early and rushed to feed and milk the cows while her mother, who was also going whelking, fed the hens and calves and when they had padded themselves with extra clothing they went together down to the shore. The other women were waiting by the dinghy.

'Will we make for the Carraig?' asked Anna Vic of Fiona's mother.

'Aye, that's the best place I'm thinkin'.'

Fiona's mother was the most expert whelk gatherer on the island and it was always left to her to say where the best picking would be. They dumped their pails and sacks into the dinghy and climbed in.

'I wish I wasn't so feared of the water,' moaned Peggy Ruag, planting herself nervously in the middle of a thwart. She giggled. 'But I'm glad to say my love of money overcomes my fear,' she admitted gaily. Fiona and Kirsty took an oar each and pulled away from the shore.

'Kirsty, what in the name of Goodness have you on

under your coat?' shrilled Anna Vic and Kirsty almost lost an oar as she tried to pull her oilskin over her bright red pyjama-covered knees. 'Why, you look as if you have the pillar box from the post office hidden there.'

Kirsty blushed. 'Indeed I never thought the day would come when I would be wearin' men's attire,' she explained apologetically. 'But I felt such cold in my legs as soon as I went outdoors this mornin' an' then when I was lookin' for somethin' warm to put on to go to the whelks I saw these an' I yielded to temptation.'

'However did you come by them?' demanded Peggy Ruag. 'An' you a woman that says she's never had a man in her life?'

'It's to that American tourist was stayin' a year or two back they rightly belong,' Kirsty told her. 'He left them behind when he went an' I never heard from him again sayin' whereabouts he was.'

The chaffing and chatter continued until after about half an hour's rowing Fiona's mother pointed to the land. 'See an' make for the rocks there,' she instructed, indicating a stretch of lonely boulder-strewn shore backed by imposing cliffs which even yet were echoing the rumbling of the previous day's storm. Fiona and Kirsty turned the boat, making for a weed-carpeted inlet between great slabs of sloping rocks and as they approached a surprised otter slid sinuously over the rocks and into the water.

'I don't like that at all,' remarked Anna Vic edgily. 'The old folk wouldn't think that was a good sign to start the whelkin'.'

'Ach, you're no believin' them tales, surely?' scoffed Peggy Ruag, alluding to the ceilidh stories of witches transforming themselves into otters to accomplish some of their ill-wishing.

'Our fathers believed it, right enough,' maintained Anna Vic.

'Aye, an' our grandfathers an' before them their grandfathers too, I daresay,' conceded Peggy. 'But to my mind the only way the otters could injure the whelkin' would be by eatin' them all before we got to them.' She chuckled. 'There's no sense in them old tales, at all,' she assured Anna Vic.

Fiona and Kirsty shipped their oars as the dinghy slid on to the tangle and the women got out and dispersed along the shore eager to begin gathering.

Fiona chose her spot and set to work. At first it was fun turning over the boulders; watching the sparks fly as they crashed against one another; smelling the sharp whiffs of brimstone; seeing the instant panic of the writhing catfish; the eruption of the newly exposed colonies of seething sandlice; the sleekly smug anemones; the spotted gunnels and the tiny green crabs scuttling for new sanctuaries, but as the limpet-encrusted rocks grated the skin from her fingers it became harsh, exacting work and she began to realize why her mother's hands were rough and insensitive as blocks of dry peat. For the first hour the whelks were scarce but as she shuffled with icy feet in pursuit of the ebbing tide they became more abundant so that instead of rattling thinly on the bottom of her pail when she threw them in she had the comfort of hearing them plop on to what had become a satisfying half pailful. But she was disappointed with her speed of picking. At this rate it was going to take the whole period of low tides to gather the five pailfuls needed to fill a hundredweight sack. Crouched down among the rocks she was effectively isolated from the other women so that she could not compare her progress with theirs and even when she straightened up to

43

flap her arms across her chest in an effort to generate some warmth into her chilled body she could see no sign of them. No doubt they were too absorbed in their whelk gathering to be conscious of the cold, she thought, and aiming to become similarly immune she hunched down, hearing nothing above the crashing of the rocks and the booming of the swell; seeing nothing but the mosaic of shingle and smashed shell uncovered by the boulders. The frosty wind burned her cheeks and glazed her eyes so that she had to blink constantly so as to distinguish the blue-black whelk shells she sought from the grey shells of dog-whelks which they so closely resembled and which, she had been told, being poisonous must be avoided at all costs. She picked on doggedly, probing beneath boulders that were too big for her to move and trying not to think of the conger eels that might be lurking beneath them ready to fasten their strong teeth into her fingers should they stray too near; trying to ignore the gripping cold; her bruised and bleeding fingers; her nails already worn down to the tender quick by the coarse shell sand among which she had to scramble for the whelks; the sea water stinging her grazes so that she was almost grateful for the desensitizing effect of the bleak wind.

She began to feel hungry but she made herself continue picking until she had a pailful of whelks before she paused to eat the damp crumbs of oatcake which were all that remained of the crisp wedge of fresh bannock she had stuffed into her pocket that morning, and as she ate she saw with concern that the tide was already beginning to creep back, licking at the shore with foaming lips and alerting the anemones to unfold their greedy fronds. Cramming the last few crumbs of oatcake into her mouth she began with renewed determination to heave over bigger and bigger boulders, scrabbling urgently for the whelks beneath as she retreated from the flowing tide and she realized with elation that her eyes, having become accustomed to the selectivity of her task, were quicker at spotting the clusters of whelks among the rocks so that her pail filled more rapidly. By the time the tide had driven her up the shore there was another half pailful to add to the two that were already in her sack. She carried her sack over to where the dinghy was moored. Her mother and the three other women were waiting for her, their tired bodies slumped against the rocks and their faces whipped to a redness that rivalled that of Kirsty's purloined pyjamas. Her mother, Fiona noticed, had picked two full hundredweight sacks of whelks; the other women had each picked more than a hundredweight.

'My, but you've done well, Fiona!' they complimented her as she dumped her sad half sackful.

She gave them a wry smile. 'I'll need to do better,' she told them.

It was growing dusk when she and her mother reached home and the hens were waiting hungrily while the cattle crowded around the door of the byre. In the kitchen the fire was out; the lamp unlit. Fiona picked up the milk pail and went outside. The soft milky teats of the cows were like balm on her smarting hands and as she rested her head against the warm comfort of their shaggy flanks great clusters of whelks swam before her tired eyes. When she went back to the house the lamp was lit and the kitchen was full of the smells of peat smoke and hot tea; of boiling potatoes and salt fish. She pulled off her gumboots and sat on the stout wooden fender, her feet pressed against the metal hob of the grate, and before she went to bed her mother softened home-made ointment in the warmth of the fire and tore strips of clean rags into bandages to protect her hands from the chafing of the rough wool blankets.

Fiona's skill at whelk gathering improved so quickly that by the end of the first period of daylight low tides she had three full sacks of whelks ready to be washed before being carried on her back the quarter of a mile up the steep brae to where the carrier would collect them.

'You'd best make halves of your bags,' Fiona's mother told her. 'It's no wise for you to carry full ones at your age.' But though she obediently made two loads of her first sack Fiona was shamed by the sight of her mother and the other women toiling up the brae with their full hundredweights. Rebelliously she roped a full sack to her shoulders and followed in their wake with desperately feigned ease. She was used to carrying heavy loads but the path was boggy and steep; the sacks dripping wet and the whelk shells pressing into her back were hard as pebbles. Before she had covered half the distance her breath was rasping against her hot throat and there was the warm salty taste of blood in her mouth. But every step was taking her nearer the dyke where the whelks would be left for collection and she was too proud to give in and take a rest. Her mother, having deposited the fourth of her eight sacks on the dyke turned and saw her daughter's struggle but instead of chiding her or going to her aid she only smiled her tired, gentle smile and turned away, pretending to examine the labels on the sacks so that Fiona should not see the glint of pride in her eyes.

'Aye well, that's done for the present,' said Peggy Ruag as she set down her last sack. Pulling back her shoulders she pressed her hands into the small of her back.

'Till the next time,' Kirsty reminded her.

They leaned against the dyke, gossiping and laughing, trying not to betray the degree of their exhaustion.

At the next daylight tides Fiona picked a further three bags of whelks and estimated that if whelk prices were as good as people were predicting she would, when she had received the money for her six bags, have sufficient to buy not only 'Janette' but perhaps a new hat also. She noticed her mother darting shrewdly enquiring glances at her from time to time and was careful to quell her growing excitement.

A month went by and the whelk gatherers, who were normally accustomed to receiving payment within a fortnight, began to question the delay. A few days later the explanation arrived in the form of a telegram. 'Send no more whelks,' it instructed. 'Market glutted. All buying ceased temporarily. Letter following.' The letter following upon the telegram brought even gloomier information. Their last two consignments had arrived at the height of the glut and as a consequence had had to be dumped.

After the first exclamations of resentment the whelk gatherers, conditioned all their lives to frustration and disappointment, accepted the situation with philosophical good humour. But since it was the first time they had known the whelk market to become glutted they repaired to Peggy Beag's cottage and drank tea while they discussed the possible reasons for the glut and mocked their presumptuous plans with hard-edged laughter.

'It was that otter,' asserted Anna Vic. 'Didn't I say at the time that it wasn't a good sign?'

'Ach, that's nonsense just,' repudiated Peggy Ruag. 'It's more likely it was those pyjamas Kirsty was wearing that put the ill luck on us.' Kirsty smiled coyly and immediately wiped the smile away with her hand.

'Or maybe it's just the fullness of the English bellies that's at the back of it,' continued Peggy.

'Maybe before the next tide they'll be wantin' whelks again,' Kirsty suggested.

'We'll take good care an' find out whether they do or not before we send them off,' Anna Vic insisted. 'Gettin' no money for our whelks is bad enough but payin' to send them to London to have them dumped is a terrible thing.'

Fiona looked across at her mother who, having gathered the largest quantity of whelks, would have the highest transport charges to pay and she knew that if the demand for whelks revived that season her first earnings would go not to buy 'Janette' but to help her mother.

'Aye well, I'd best be away,' said Anna Vic. She stood in the open doorway looking out across the sea. 'I was thinkin' maybe with the money from the whelks I would get a bit of waxcloth for the floor,' she told them. 'What's down now is as full of holes as a cod net.' She giggled. 'I wouldn't care for ourselves but for my cousin that's comin' from Glasgow in the spring.'

'Aye, right enough, you could do with it,' Peggy Ruag told her. 'When folks come from Glasgow they think if you haven't a bit of waxcloth on the floor you're livin' in a pig sty.'

'We all had our plans, I doubt,' interposed Kirsty quietly.

'Plans?' echoed Peggy Beag. 'What wasn't I plannin' to buy? Why, I was for gettin' one of them pressure lamps that gives such a lovely light, an' I was for gettin' some new overalls the way I'd look more respectable when the minister comes. I even thought at one time I might get one of them fancy quilts for my bed.' She bubbled over with derisive laughter.

'Was the new quilt for when the minister comes too?' Anna Vic shrilled.

'Oh, the Dear!' remonstrated Kirsty, sucking back a threatening smile.

Neither Fiona nor her mother referred to the subject of the dumped whelks and in her candlelit bedroom that night Fiona stuffed the mail order catalogue into one of the boxes under her bed. She wouldn't be needing that for a while, she told herself and for a few moments she let her body sag with dejection. She looked at the grazed skin of her hands and thought of the hours she had laboured in the bitter cold and of the racking burden of the dripping sacks of whelks as she had carried them up the brae. She leaned her elbows on the chest beneath the tiny window of her room and stared at the dark peaks of the hills where silver ribbons of cloud were stretched tight across the rising moon. She turned away, shrugging her shoulders. Oh well, she told herself. There'll come another season. Another whelk gathering.

## The Lonely Ghost

'I'm not claiming I saw a ghost,' I insisted. 'All I am saying is that I saw a man coming to my house three hours after you say he was dead.'

My assertion brought tolerant grunts from the men and whispers of disquiet from the women who were assembled at the evening ceilidh. Lachlan solemnly knocked out his pipe on the bars of the grate and Ian, with equal solemnity, spat into the fire. We all stared with varying degrees of interest at the glob of spittle shrivelling on the glowing peat.

'He was dead, right enough,' maintained Erchy.

'Indeed that's true,' asseverated Morag. 'Wasn't myself there with Barbac and Murdoch waitin' beside the bed for the last wind to go out of him just. An' didn't Murdoch lean over the bed to say somethin' when his teeths fell out an' slid off the bed down on to the floor. I bent down to get a hold of them before anyone would put a foot on them an' I'd scarce raised myself again when Neilly was gone.'

'Why had Murdoch got his teeths in?' interrupted Johnny.

'Ach, to see Neilly off just,' explained Morag. 'An' the nurse was there straightenin' him out before nine o'clock,' she concluded with emphasis.

'There now!' said Janet, summing up the evidence. 'Whoever it was you saw last night it couldn't have been Neilly himself.'

'It was a ghost you saw, surely,' said Anna Vic.

Of course I hadn't seen a ghost. The man I had seen was flesh and blood and I would have sworn to that. But then I would also have sworn that the man I had seen the previous evening was none other than the dead Neilly. It had been coming up to nine o'clock and a damp chill dusk was beginning to soak into the evening. I had been over to the henhouse to ensure my broody hen was back on her nest and to close up the hens for the night and I was just about to go inside my cottage when I caught sight of Neilly coming along the path. I had no doubts that it was Neilly: Bruach's population was small enough for each inhabitant to be easily recognizable even at considerable distances and Neilly was no more than fifty yards away. I knew him by his gait; by his size and shape; by the peaked yachtsman's cap he always wore and by the fact that he was smoking a cigarette. Though most of the young men in Bruach smoked cigarettes all the old men remained pipe addicts; all that is except Neilly who was the only man of his generation to have acquired the habit of cigarette smoking. As I waited by the open door I saw his cigarette glow bright as if he had taken a strong puff at it and then the next moment he had thrown it aside. In the dusk I saw the red ash scatter over the grass and I was about to call out to him when he had turned abruptly and gone away. After a moment of surprise I had shrugged my shoulders and thought no more of the incident. Neilly had not previously ventured near my cottage except once to bring me a telegram and I assumed that having seen that I was alone he had suddenly changed his mind about coming to see me. Consequently the next morning when Erchy had called out to me in passing that Neilly was dead I was genuinely shocked.

'That's very sudden!' I exclaimed.

'Aye, sudden enough,' agreed Erchy. He was on his way to lift his lobster creels at the time so I did not delay him with questions. Nor did I mention that I had seen Neilly only the previous evening so when, at the ceilidh that night, someone mentioned his having died 'at the back of six' I had immediately disputed the time, explaining that it was impossible for Neilly to have been dead at six o'clock when I had seen him, presumably still hale and hearty, at nine o'clock.

'I know it was round nine o'clock,' I assured them, 'because when I went inside I put on the wireless and listened to the news.' I did not know then that Neilly had been too ill to rise from his bed for three days before he died so it was natural that their reaction to my claim to have seen him at any time at all the previous evening should be one of mingled disbelief and consternation.

'If you didn't see a ghost then who was it you saw?' persisted Anna Vic, who would never have risked hurting my feelings by suggesting that I had been mistaken.

I shook my head slowly. 'I don't know,' I said. 'Obviously it wasn't Neilly but I'm blessed if I know who it was in that case.'

'Then it was someone mighty like,' said Erchy.

'He must have been or I wouldn't have made the mistake,' I agreed.

'Ach, but maybe you were not mistaken at all,' speculated Anna Vic.

'Aye, right enough I believe she might have had the second sight if she'd not been born in a town,' said Erchy, scrutinizing me with much the same interest as a pathologist might scrutinize a specimen in a bottle.

'I certainly haven't got second sight,' I denied with a smile.

Lachlan spoke 'You say he was smokin' a cigarette?' he probed. I nodded and they thought for a while, murmuring interrogatively but not, I thought, so much interested in whether or not I had seen a ghost as Anna Vic wanted to surmise but in the more practical question as to who it could have been coming to visit me? Why would he be coming? Why had he changed his mind and gone away again? The obvious answer was that whoever it had been had wanted to borrow something but they could think of no one who was currently proposing to embark on any job for which he might need to borrow tools from me and, of course it was unthinkable that it could have been anyone wanting to return something already borrowed. In Bruach when you lent anything you usually had to follow its track round from neighbour to neighbour when you wanted it back.

'What like of man would go that close to a place an' then turn away without so much as a word?' demanded Adam, the gamekeeper, in a puzzled voice. 'Nobody from hereabouts surely?'

'Indeed no,' endorsed Janet. 'An' there's been no stranger here for weeks past.'

'It's the cigarette that is the mystery,' pronounced Lachlan. 'Indeed I know of no man who could look like Neilly an' be smokin' a cigarette.'

'Well, I did mention that he threw it away,' I reminded them but they ignored me and again fell to discussing the possible identity of the man I claimed to have seen. Each suggestion was rejected almost as quickly as it was offered.

'It's strange if it was Neilly when you come to think of it,' Janet pointed out. 'It's not as though you've ever had much to do with the man since you've been here.'

'That's true,' I agreed. I had had very little to do with Neilly. Like everyone else we commented politely on the weather by way of greeting whenever we met but since Neilly rarely dropped in at any of the ceilidhs and since he did not shop at the grocery van or join up with the peat cutting parties in spring there was really no common meeting place. The only time I had exchanged more than half a dozen consecutive words with him was one day when I had been coming back from an early morning wander on the moors. I had been picking my way around the peat bogs when I heard a shout and looking in the direction from which it came I saw Neilly's wife, Barbac, sitting beside the road. She was clutching at her stomach and had obviously been vomiting but she insisted that she was all right except that when the vomiting struck her first she had fallen and twisted her knee so that now she 'couldn't put her leg under her'. Would I go and get Neilly, she pleaded. It was over a mile across the moors to Neilly's house and when I reached it I was both breathless and flustered. Neilly was cleaning out the calf shed and I rushed towards him but the moment he saw me making in his direction he rushed inside the shed and shut the door. Fuming at his shyness I stood outside the door and bawled, 'For goodness' sake come out,' I told him. 'It's your wife.'

The door opened cautiously and Neilly appeared still holding the graipe which he had been using to throw out the manure. 'My wife is away milkin' the cow,' he told me.

'I know that,' I panted. 'But she's sick. And she's twisted her leg.'

'Oh, my, my! That's terrible!' Neilly's face was full of concern and he dug his graipe hurriedly into the ground. 'I'd best be away up to the post office an' try will I catch the vet before he's out on his rounds,' he said.

'Not the vet!' I told him breathlessly. 'It's your wife who's needing attention.'

'Oh, it's no the cow that's sick then?' Neilly's relief was staggeringly obvious. 'It's my wife, you say?'

'Yes,' I stressed. 'She's twisted her leg somehow and she cannot walk. She's also been vomiting quite a lot and I'm afraid she's going to get very cold sitting out there on the moor. We must get help to her as quickly as possible.' I found I was still shouting at him, I was so repelled by his attitude now that he knew his cow was safe. 'Would you like me to go up to the post office and telephone for the nurse while you go to your wife?' I asked him. 'It wouldn't take her long to get here and she could bring your wife home in her car.'

'The nurse is on holiday,' Neilly informed me almost exultantly. 'You would need to get the nurse from the next village an' it would be an hour or more before she would get here.'

I looked at him defiantly. 'I think I ought to telephone her all the same,' I said.

Neilly surveyed me with a calmness of expression that implied I was making a great deal of fuss over nothing at all. 'You could do that if you've a mind,' he conceded. 'An' I will get one or two of the men and we will take the bier for her. That will be the way of it just.' I made no comment. There were times when I thought Bruach would have been bereft without its funeral bier; it was put to such a variety of uses that I used to wonder why each crofter did not have one of his own. Returning from telephoning the nurse I was in time to see the rescue party setting off across the moors but looking ahead of them I also saw to my utter dismay that Barbac herself was already half way home! She had felt fine when she had done vomiting, she told me later and when her knee had suddenly 'jumped back into its bones' she had carried on, milked the cow, and was on her way home when she had met the bier bearers. Barbac had subsequently professed herself grateful for my efforts to help but Neilly never made any secret of the fact that ne despised me for the fuss I had made.

'I'm no understandin' it at all,' said Anna Vic. 'You'd think a man that has kept away from you in life would keep away from you in death,' she added.

'There's not many it could have been, all the same,' said Tearlaich with a puzzled frown. 'We was all away diggin' his grave.'

'An' them that was no diggin' was after sittin' with the corpse,' declared Erchy.

There was a long pause during which Janet placed more peats on the fire and brushed some ash from the hearth with a bundle of feathers. Then Morag said, 'There's some believes it takes a spirit three days to make up its mind where it's goin'.'

Erchy and Johnny flicked her a surprised look but said nothing.

'If they ever go at all rightly,' said Lachlan.

'Like Red Annie?' asked Anna Vic.

'Like Red Annie,' agreed Lachlan. We knew we had only to relax now and stare into the fire while we waited for Lachlan to tell us the story of Red Annie. For the Bruachites no doubt it would be the umpteenth time they had heard it but for me Red Annie was still a stranger.

'Poor Red Annie,' began Lachlan. 'Aye, she was young to go when she did.' He took down a tin of baking soda from the mantelpiece and swallowed two teaspoonfuls before he took up the narrative again. 'No more than twenty was she on the day she died. She was on her way back from yon village with a boll of meal an' a hundred-weight of coarse salt roped to her back when it started to snow. Not heavy snow, mind, at first, but it was gettin' thicker all the time an' with the weight she had there was no tellin' how it was holdin' her back. No doubt she was makin' herself believe if she kept goin' she would be back before the night came down but with nine miles walked an' another three still to go the struggle got too much for her an' she burst her own heart. That's the way they

57

found her two days later, with the meal still roped to her back. My own father was one that went out to look for her an' it was himself told me that.'

There were small murmurs of compassion from the women as they thought of the young red-haired Annie struggling through the blizzard only to collapse and die three miles away from her home.

'It was a lonely way to die,' said Anna Vic sadly.

'Aye, an' I'm thinkin' it's lonely she is to this day,' continued Lachlan. 'Why else would there be nothin' but bracken will grow on the good land where she died?' He looked around, inviting contradiction.

I, visualizing the road to Bruach and recalling no part of it that was lush enough to grow bracken, was unable to locate the particular spot where Red Annie was supposed to have died. At length I had to ask.

'It's no place on the road as you would know it, Miss Peckwitt,' Lachlan explained. 'This was back in my father's time an' the road then was higher up the hill.'

'It used to go above the strath, over the shoulder of the hill,' interjected Erchy. 'You can still make out part of the old track.'

'Aye, an' if you look up there you will see in the middle of the good land there is a patch of bracken growin' all to itself,' said Lachlan, taking up the story again.

'I have noticed that,' I said, remembering the isolated circle of bracken among the greenness of the laird's parkland. I had often pondered over the reason for its being there and wished that it had not been 'estate land' so that I could have climbed up to investigate it. 'But why is it included in the laird's park now?' I asked.

'Ach, when the new laird came he just told us he was goin' to take the road down nearer the shore. He said it would be easier for us and I'm no sayin' but that he wasn't right but at the same time he took where the road had once been into his own park.' Lachlan nodded wisely. 'He might as well have left it,' he went on, 'for once he'd moved the road it seemed nothin' but bracken would ever grow on the patch where Red Annie died, though there'd been good grazin' there before. He even planted it with trees but he could never get them to cover that spot, just. He reckoned it was a kind of a wind funnel that killed everythin',' Lachlan added with a wry grunt. 'But to my my own mind it was cursed.'

I was still trying to sort out the implication of Lachlan's story when the door opened and Angy the fisherman came bringing in the fresh smell of the sea on his oilskins. I waited for the greetings to cease before I put to Lachlan the question that was puzzling me.

'This story of Red Annie,' I taxed him. 'Do you mean that nothing will grow on that particular spot because she died there?'

'Indeed no,' responded Lachlan. 'It is not that at all. It is because the laird moved the road away from where she died that nothin' will grow there, you understand?'

I didn't understand and I suppose it was obvious from my expression.

'What I'm sayin' is that a person's spirit or ghost if you like always stays around the place where he died,' expounded Lachlan patiently. 'An' so long as it has company the same as it had in life then it will no be a trouble to anyone at all. That patch of land where Red Annie died stayed good land so long as her spirit had the company of folks that was passin' along the road. But when the laird moved the road then that was the time for things to change.'

'You mean Annie's ghost became lonely?'

'Just that.' He nodded approval at me. 'That's what we believe, anyway,' he added.

'Didn't anyone try to dissuade the laird from moving the road?' I asked.

'They tried. Right enough they tried but he wouldn't listen to them at all. He thought he was doin' them good by savin' them havin' to climb so high up the hill.'

'But nobody told him why they didn't want the road to be moved,' Tearlaich said accusingly.

'How would they tell him an' him an Englishman?' retorted Lachlan.

'Aye well,' said Johnny. 'I'm mighty glad he did change the road. I wouldn't want to take my bus that far up the hill. It's plenty bad enough without that.'

I was too interested in Lachlan's theory to let the subject drop. 'Do you think then that all these haunted places we hear about are haunted simply because whoever is haunting them is missing company?' I pursued.

'Surely if the ghost gives trouble that would be the reason for it likely,' he replied. 'Maybe there was never any trouble until the place had been deserted for a while but once a ghost's been left on its own it gets kind of vexed about it an' maybe tries to get a bit of its own back by plaguin' folks.'

Lachlan pushed his pipe into his mouth and taking the hint I ceased my questioning.

'Well, I'm thinkin' Neilly's goin' to be a sore miss to Barbac,' said Morag piously.

'Aye, right enough,' concurred Angy. 'When are you buryin' him?' Angy fished from a mainland port and came home only at weekends so that he was not as well acquainted with Bruach affairs as were the rest.

'Monday,' Erchy told him.

'Hell, you're for keepin' him long enough,' Angy expostulated. 'He'll be smellin' by Monday.'

'What do you care?' demanded Tearlaich. 'You won't have to carry him. You'll be away at sea again by then likely.'

'Aye, thank God!' retaliated Angy. He lit a cigarette. 'As a matter of fact we had a death on board our own boat today. That's why I'm in so early.'

'Who was that?' asked Morag.

'Ach, no one you'd be knowin'. It was a fellow that hasn't been with us for long.'

'How did he die?'

'He just collapsed,' Angy said. 'The way of it was there was a big kick in the tides today an' we had to rush off down to the harbour for fear of missin' it. This fellow was keepin' up with the rest of us all right then as soon as we got aboard he just crumpled up an' died.' Angy seemed to enjoy the shocked expressions on our faces.

'It would be his heart likely?' asked Janet.

'Aye, I would think it couldn't be much else,' agreed Angy.

'So you didn't get your day's fishin' after all your rushin',' observed Erchy.

'Indeed we did,' Angy assured him. 'An' a good day's fishin' it was too for all we were in early.'

'You were lucky then,' Erchy told him. 'I would think you'd be kept back with the doctor an' everybody wantin' to ask you what happened.'

'Ach, we didn't wait for all that,' said Angy.

'You surely didn't take a dead man to sea with you?' challenged Janet in an outraged voice.

'We did not then,' Angy told her. 'What we did was

wrap him up in a piece of tarpaulin we had aboard an' then four of us carried him up to the fish store between us.'

'You put him in the fish store?' Anna Vic squeaked.

'Aye, there was a slab there handy, you see. An' there was some of these labels they put on the fish boxes, so we just wrote on a couple of them an' stuck them on the tarpaulin.'

'An' what did you say on the labels?' asked Erchy.

' "To be delivered",' said Angy. 'I believe that's what they usually say.'

'Oh, hear!' whispered Janet.

'You didn't even straighten the man out?' exclaimed Morag.

'I tell you there was no time. We were near missin' the tide as it was.' Angy was entirely unabashed.

'Whatever would the fish salesman say when he came to unwrap what he would think would be a good catch of fish an' finds a corpse just?' asked Anna Vic. Angy only shrugged. 'An' what would they do with him supposin' they found him?'

'I don't know an' I don't care.' Angy was becoming impatient. 'All I know is they'd find him all right. We left him in a place where they couldn't miss him.'

'Where was that?' asked Morag.

'Didn't I tell you, on the fish slab itself,' retorted Angy. 'An' since they'd need to have the slab clear before they started filletin' the fish they'd have to do somethin' with him. They wouldn't just leave him there.'

I found myself swallowing rather hard.

'The poor man!' breathed Morag.

'Ach, he wasn't much of a fellow,' said Angy dismissively. 'He was only a fisherman because he couldn't keep another job an' he was nothin' but a bloody landlubber aboard. Honest, he was so scared of the sea he couldn't pee from the time we left the harbour till the time we got back in again.'

I stood up. 'It's time I was away home to my bed,' I announced. There was a general move to go and as we stood outside assessing the night before we took our different paths Erchy said, I suspected with the intention of frightening me, 'I'd like fine to know whether it was Neilly's ghost you saw last night.'

'Ach, how could it have been?' asked Tearlaich. 'What would Neilly be wantin' from Miss Peckwitt?'

'Did you say it was about nine o'clock when you saw him?' Erchy would not leave the subject alone.

'Yes,' I said resignedly.

'Then I doubt he was wantin' in to have a listen to the news on the wireless,' said Erchy.

'More like to listen to the weather forecast,' put in Johnny. 'He'd be wantin' to know what like of weather he was goin' to get for his own funeral.'

# The Shenagelly

I had been over to the mainland and had finished all my business there several hours before the bus was due to return to Bruach and since the inducements to linger on the mainland were limited to the chilly railway station buffet and the equally chilly local tearoom, both of which offered identical fare and provided identical comfort, i.e.

tea and stale cake and straight-backed wooden benches I
resolved to begin walking back to Bruach and to take the
opportunity of calling in on a friend who lived close to the
bus route. When I set out it was a pleasant afternoon in
November, cold and clear except for the tendrils of mist
which a lisping wind was curling round the crook-backed
hills. The wide moors, gashed by the black troughs of peat
diggings, stretched on either side of the road and there
was no sound save that of my own footsteps; the occasional
'clunk' of a raven; the mewing of a buzzard and from
somewhere in the hills the echoing bleating of sheep. My
friend's house was about six miles away and before I had
covered five miles I had seen the tendrils of mist spread,
densen and merge to enfold all but the skirt edges of the
hills and the sky greying to release a thin drizzle of chilly
rain. I was beginning to grow tired of walking but I
quickened my step, thinking of my friend's warm bright
kitchen and of the strupak which would undoubtedly be
prepared for me there. However as I approached the
house I began to suspect I might be in for a disappointment. There was no smoke eddying round the chimney
and as I opened the gate I saw with some surprise that the
door of the house was tight shut. I turned the handle and
poking my head inside called out, 'Are you there, Marie?'
The only response was an inarticulate croak from the
direction of the fireplace where an old man sat like a fossil
in a wooden chair beside the sluggish peat fire. I recalled
Marie having told me about a ninety-year-old uncle of
hers who was coming to live with her and guessed that
this was he.

'He Fluke,' I said. The old man only stared at me
warily without moving his lips. I assumed he was deaf and
shouted my greeting. 'He Fluke.' He nodded but his 'He

Fluke' in return was reluctant and barely audible. I stepped inside and he shrank back in his chair. 'Is Marie not at home?' I asked and then repeated my question in a louder voice.

'Ha Nyall!' His voice was thick and his faded old eyes wide with apprehension.

I moved towards a chair and sat down.

The fire was piled with dry peats but only a wisp of smoke was threading its way round them and I wondered if I dared offer to set the fire blazing again by pushing in some of the dry twigs which lay ready on the hearth.

'Is Marie about the croft?' I asked. I had to shout the question three times before he understood it and each time I leaned forward to shout he cringed further and further away from me.

'Ha Nyall!' he muttered and then in a slightly more confident voice added, 'The doctor.'

My heart sank. If Marie had gone to see the doctor then in all probability she would be returning on the very bus which I had to catch. I realized it was no use waiting. There was no welcome for me here for though the old man was ninety, almost stone deaf and crippled with rheumatism he was obviously so scared of my being a stranger that I feared he might die of fright if I stayed.

'Oidche Mhath!' I called defeatedly as I closed the door behind me.

'Oidche Mhath!' The reply came with an instant of animation. It was beginning to grow dark; lamplight glowed behind the misted windows of the croft houses and as I walked on through the scattered village I debated what I should do. The cold had not worried me hitherto but now after my rebuff at Marie's cottage I was aware that my hands and feet were really very cold; that my

66

clothes felt clammy and that my legs were aching with weariness, yet the bus was not due for at least another two hours. Once I had left the village behind there would be no more houses; no shelter of any kind; not even the faintest glimmer of light to be discerned until I came in sight of Bruach while the road itself as it began to wind its way through night-soaked hills would grow steadily darker and eerier. I had taken a torch with me to the mainland intending to get new batteries for it but alas I was informed there was a shortage of batteries so my empty torch lay uselessly at the bottom of my bag. I thought of seeking shelter at one of the croft houses, knowing that I had only to ask and not just shelter but a welcome strupak would be immediately forthcoming but I also knew from my own experience that this hour, just when dusk is closing in over the land, is always the busiest one of the crofter's day and I was loath to burden them with the company of a stranger.

I was passing the last house in the village and with the prospect of the lonely dark road confronting me had more or less decided to overcome my reservations and ask for shelter when I glimpsed an unfamiliar light on my left. With a surge of relief I suddenly remembered there had been talk at one of the ceilidhs about Hamish having recently opened a shop in the shed he had built at the end of his house. 'Someone else that's after thinkin' he'll make money out of us,' Erchy had said gloomily. I stared at the light only half believing my good luck and then I hurried towards it fearful lest it should disappear leaving me to face once more the decision as to whether I should go on or go back.

I turned the handle of the shop door and went inside. Hamish was leaning on the counter reading a magazine and when he looked up and saw me his surprise was so great his spectacles fell on to the counter.

'He Fluke!' I greeted him.

'He Fluke!' he replied with a worried frown that was intended as a disguise for his diffidence.

Hamish was known as the 'Shenagelly' which Morag translated for me as being a 'man that doesn't take lightly to women', and I knew him, as he knew me, by sight and reputation only. He was a gangling man, clumsy with shyness and seeing that I intended he and his shop should endure my presence for the next couple of hours I set about putting him at his ease.

'My, but you have a splendid little store here,' I complimented him as I surveyed his crammed and varied stock of tinned fruit, biscuits, sweeties, butter, flour, crockery, paint, nails, brushes, soap and cigarettes along with what seemed to me a disproportionate quantity of aspirin tablets.

'Ach!' He waved his hand in a deprecating gesture. 'I've more than this coming.' He nodded towards the road. 'Johnny's bringing me a box of gumboots when he comes.' He looked down at my sodden shoes. 'Ladies' boots, too,' he added.

I too looked down at my shoes. 'My gumboots are on the bus,' I explained. 'I've been over to the mainland and when I'd finished there I decided to walk back to Bruach. It was a nice enough day when I started out.'

Hamish was aghast. 'You've walked all that way?' he asked. 'Did you no stop any place?' I told him of my plan to drop in and see Marie and of finding the old man there alone and aloof. 'My, my,' he commiserated. 'You'll not have had a strupak since you left the mainland, then?'

'I'm not so much missing a strupak as wanting to sit

down,' I told him. 'I wonder would you mind if I sat down on the end of this box while I give you my order?' I indicated a large wooden crate labelled 'CANDLES'.

'Ach, this one's best,' said Hamish. 'That one's wet with the dogs.' He bumbled forward and gathered up some tins so that I could sit down on a box that was clearly marked 'DO NOT CRUSH'.

'Lovely,' I said, easing myself down. It was only fractionally warmer inside the shop than outside but at least it was dry and I was comfortable enough as I made my choice of the items he had to offer. When I had paid for my purchases and had stowed them away in my bag I began to cast around for an interesting topic of conversation but Hamish began to clear his throat nervously, and then burst out, 'Will you take a strupak supposing I make one?' I told him of course that it would be putting him to too much trouble but he must have read the longing in my expression.

'It is not very nice for you to be sitting in the cold here,' he told me and indicated the door that led through to his house. 'If you will come with me just through here I will show you my private parts.' Unhesitatingly I followed him. I had heard that Hamish had made himself a 'swanky' home and I was struck by the difference between it and the usual crofter's house. Here were comfortable armchairs; a writing desk; a polished table, even a square of carpet on the floor. The house smelled of furniture polish instead of the usual mixture of hens' mash, sour milk and peat smoke and when he turned up the jet of the gaslight the sheen on the woodwork showed how much attention was lavished on it. I enthused on its appearance while Hamish filled a kettle from the pail of water, for despite his modern furniture and the convenience of bottled gas he still had to carry all his water from the well. He set the kettle on a small gas ring.

'If you would care to blow up the fire,' he told me, indicating an extremely functional pair of bellows, 'I will get some biscuits from out the shop.' Contentedly I went down on my knees and worked the bellows until the flames burst and spread themselves over the dry peats. When Hamish returned he threw on some chunks of driftwood and some pieces of coal.

'I have closed the shop,' he told me, setting down the hurricane lantern which had provided light for the shop. 'There will be no one coming now and we can see the headlights of the bus from the window in plenty of time.'

It was so long since I had been entertained in such a charming room and as I sat toasting my feet and drinking hot tea I reflected on my good fortune. Over his strupak Hamish became almost loquacious, telling me of his early life on the mainland. He was, as I suspected, no High-lander: to me he did not even look like one, but his maternal grandmother had been a Highlander and through her he had inherited the croft; his passionate love of the island, and presumably his Highland way of speech. Our talk turned to writing and he confessed that some-times he wrote poetry; he suggested that I might like him to read some of his poems to me and I, feeling so smug and warm that I could have listened to a party political broadcast without flinching, expressed keen interest. He took a sheaf of papers from the writing desk and started to read in a flat voice that would have ruined a Shake-spearean sonnet while all the time he fidgeted so extrava-gantly – crossing and uncrossing legs and drawing first one knee up to his chin and then the other – that it was evident what the reading of them was costing him. It occurred to me that he must be a very lonely man, being as he was a non-Highlander among Highlanders; a non-crofter among crofters, for though Hamish had inherited the croft it was only the house which interested him. He kept no animals and grew no crops. He did not even cut peats for himself but resorted to buying a few sacks from his neighbours when he wanted to eke out his coal. I knew what it was like to be an Englishwoman among Highlanders (though once when I had mentioned this to Morag she had dismissed the idea of my place of birth being of any moment – 'If you had been born in a stable it wouldn't have made you a horse', she had quoted). But at least I was a crofter so that I shared and could discuss the demands and frustrations, the rewards and compensations, of the crofting life with my neighbours. I began to suspect that perhaps Hamish had opened his shop not so much with the idea of making a profit from the village as of making contact with the people and I felt a wave of pity for him.

When he had finished reading his poems he relapsed into a thoughtful silence. I looked at my watch. There was still half an hour to go at least before I could expect to see the headlights of the bus and since we had finished our strupaks I suggested I should wash the dishes. I expected him to refuse politely but Hamish seemed delighted by my offer and poured the remainder of the water from the kettle into a bowl. While I washed he wiped the dishes and put them away.

'It is the first time in many years since a woman has washed dishes for me,' he confided and there was a tinge of sadness in his voice.

We sat down again to wait and again I remarked on the

attractiveness of his home. 'You know, Hamish,' I told him, 'You really should get married. It seems such a pity that such a lovely place as you have should be wasted on a bachelor.'

Hamish's eyes lit up and he looked at me shyly. 'It's funny you should say that,' he began. I saw that he was blushing fiercely and once again he began contorting himself on his chair. 'You see, I've been suffering from terrible headaches for a good while now.' He cleared his throat several times. 'I've been taking these aspirins night after night to try will it cure them; sometimes during the day too but then my head was getting so bad I couldn't sleep at all so I went with it to the doctor a week or two back.' Hamish looked straight at me. 'He told me just the same you are telling me. "You should get married, Hamish," says he. "It's only marriage will cure your headaches." '

'Really!' I murmured.

'Yes,' he admitted. 'He said that was my only cure.'

The rising wind flung a scatter of hail against the window and the suddenness of it made us glance at one another. I hoped the smile I gave Hamish was as reassuring and guileless as the smile he gave me. 'Then we can expect to hear of wedding bells in the not too distant future,' I said. I saw his eyes flick to the window and turning glimpsed the headlights of the bus glaring through the darkness.

Three months later I received an invitation to Hamish's wedding.

'Him that's been so feared of women all these years an' now he's in that much of a hurry to get married you'd think someone was after beatin' him into it!' exclaimed Morag disapprovingly. 'What will he be doin' with a

wife anyway when he has no cattle nor even a hen to see
to.'

I smiled as I put the invitation back on the shelf. 'I'm
only wondering what he's going to do with all that
aspirin,' I told her.

## The New Boots

It was seven o'clock and the December morning was a
welter of wind and rain and flung spray. Katac crouched
in the forepeak of Angus Mhor's boat as it punched its
way across the tossing black water of the sound towards
the tiny creek where she could land and so begin the
second stage of her journey to the mainland.

'You'll need to be jumpin' for it, I'm thinkin',' Angus Mhor's voice reached her from the stern. 'The swell is breakin' too close to the shore for me to go right in.'

There was no real landing place at the creek they were making for, only a cleared shingle-floored gully between piled boulders and except in the calmest weather it was possible only to nose the bow of a boat as far as the most seaward boulders when the passengers would jump from the forepeak and hope to land, if not on the shingle, then in water shallow enough not to fill their boots. Katac was in no way alarmed at the prospect of having to jump even on to a shore unlit by anything more effective than the wavering beam of Angus's torch but she was worried in case the sea came over the top of her gumboots and wet her stockings. Today it was important that she should not get her stockings wet.

'Get yourself ready, Katac!' Angus warned. Katac tightened the tapes of her souwester, checked the knot of the rope which was tied round her waist over her father's old oilskin, picked up her bag and climbed up on to the forepeak, holding on to the mast while her eyes probed the darkness trying to discern the line of the shore. Angus slowed the engine and she saw the white line of surf and the wet shingle reflecting the beam of his torch. She waited while the sea surged past the bow of the boat, flung itself at the rocks and sucked back with a clatter of stones.

'Now!' yelled Angus and immediately Katac leapt, landed on shingle, picked herself up and scrambled quickly out of the way of the next surge. At the top of the tide she stood gasping.

'All right?' she heard Angus's voice faintly.

'All right, Angus,' she called and pulling the torch out

of her bag she flashed it twice – the pre-arranged signal to indicate that she had landed without mishap. The acknowledging two flashes came from the boat and were followed by the noise of the propellor thrashing the water as Angus turned and headed back for the island.

Katac sought the shelter of a pillar of rock while she stood for a few moments watching the mast light bobbing and swaying into the dark. She wriggled her toes inside her boots. Sometimes her gumboots were so damp she wouldn't notice an extra splash or two of water in them but, she smiled to herself, today she was confident she had managed to keep her feet dry.

In the light of her torch she picked her way over the shingle towards the steep path which led to the road and the scattering of croft houses which comprised the village. The wind was strengthening, tearing at her oilskin while the rain rattled deafeningly against her souwester. She began to worry that it might grow too stormy for the ferry to cross to the mainland.

Outside the cottage which was also the village post office she sheltered in the lee of a convenient peat stack beside the road from where through the rain she glimpsed the fitful glare of headlights as the bus wound its way round the loch. It was not long before it came labouring up the hill to stop outside the post office. Although it was always referred to as the bus it was in reality no more than a covered lorry whose primary function was the collection of mails from the outlying villages and houses for delivery to the sorting office some twenty miles away. Passengers were a secondary consideration, the only concession to their comfort being the provision of two long wooden benches, one on either side of the lorry, but since these benches were not secured in any way and the rough road was full of twists and turns, Hamish, the driver, thought-fully saw that the sacks of mails were dumped on the floor between the two benches so when the lorry lurched or swooped to left or right the full sacks acted as a buffer between the two rows of dislodged passengers.

Katac stepped out from behind the peat stack into the beam of the headlights. Hamish got down from his cab. 'Ach, it is yourself, Katac,' he greeted her. 'Are you for comin' on the bus, then?'

'I am so,' she told him.

'Aye, then seein' there's no likely to be any other passengers you might just as well sit yourself in the seat beside me.' He opened the door of the cab. 'See an' get in just an' be out of the rain while I get the mails.'

He ran into the post office and Katac slipped off her oilskin before climbing into the cab. Once seated she took off her gumboots, replacing them with her best hill boots which she had been carrying in her bag. From her bag also she took her hat which she normally wore only on the Sabbath and after pulling it into shape she set it carefully on her head.

'Ach, it is terrible weather,' panted Hamish as he jumped into the driving seat after having stowed the mails in the back of the lorry. 'I'm thinkin' all the islands will be sailin' away from the mainland with all the rain there's been just.'

Katac smiled her reply. The bus started with a jolt that set her well back on her seat and knocked her hat askew. She adjusted it hastily and settled herself more firmly into her seat while her thoughts roamed over the day ahead.

Today was her twelfth birthday and this was her first journey alone to the mainland. Such trips were rare enough even with her mother, and it was eighteen months

77

since she had seen a shop of any kind, their small island boasting only a post office which was really no more than a couple of littered shelves in Marie Bheag's kitchen. Under the stolid calm she was affecting Katac was wildly excited not only by the prospect of a day's shopping but because today she was to collect a pair of birthday present boots from Old Donald, the cobbler. It would be the first time she had ever had a birthday present from her parents and what was more important it would be the first time she had ever had a pair of light boots. For months now she had been looking forward to her new boots and when walking sedately to church between her mother and father she had sometimes found herself glancing surreptitiously down at her feet and seeing in imagination not the well polished but heavy hill boots which her father deemed the only suitable footwear for girls of her age, but the shiny black, light boots which today she was going to possess.

As the bus rounded the loch she could feel the strong wind buffeting the lorry and she began again to worry lest the ferry might not be able to cross. Hamish's voice broke into her thoughts.

'You will be doin' some shopping?' he asked.

'Aye,' she replied.

'Are you goin' across?'

'I hope so,' she said, struggling to keep the anxiety out of her voice.

'Ach, you'll get across all right,' Hamish assured her. 'This sou-westerly isn't bad over the other side.'

Katac relaxed. Hamish knew a lot about winds and tides and how they affected the ferry so he wasn't likely to be wrong. The bus lumbered on while Hamish chatted sporadically about the weather or the poaching or the fishing; stopping at the home-made red painted pillar boxes which stood at the entrance to each isolated croft where he collected mails and parcels and threw them into the back of the lorry. Once a dark shape loomed grotesquely in the headlights and when Hamish stopped Katac saw it was an oilskinned and oil-coated fisherman who handed Hamish two parcels of fish, telling him there was one for himself and requesting that the other be delivered to another cottage further inland.

'I'm no askin' what it is,' jested Hamish.

The fisherman looked at Katac and winked before he merged again into the darkness.

Next it was an old woman they had to stop for, and Katac noticed that though she carried an oilskin it was draped over a bag of fleece while her own shoulders were protected by nothing more rain-proofed than an empty sack. Again it was an old man who signalled them to stop by brandishing a couple of rabbits in the headlights and once more it was with a 'one for yourself, Hamish', along with the instruction that the other should be delivered to some relative in the next village. Another time they had to stop for a cow which had chosen to bed itself down in the middle of the road and unaffected by the revving of the bus engine or by long blasts on the horn refused to move until Hamish at last got out and belaboured the beast with empty mail bags and a selection of epithets.

'The rain seems to be easin' off,' he said, getting back into his seat. Katac was relieved. She was by no means daunted by rain but in the islands rain was such a constant accompaniment that it was pleasant to be without it on occasion.

The dawn was threading itself between the peaks of the mainland hills before the bus eventually stopped at the post office where the mail was to be delivered. Katac bundled her gumboots and souwester inside her oilskin and asked Hamish to look after them until she returned with the bus that evening.

'Do you think you may be needin' them before the day is out?' he asked her with mock concern since he knew that away from their own small territory no respectable islander would care to be seen in such attire no matter what the weather.

'Indeed no.' There was a trace of indignation in Katac's chuckle. 'I wore those to save my own clothes comin' over in the boat just,' she told him. She jumped down.

'Aye, well now see an' don't be missin' the bus back now,' teased Hamish.

'I'll mind,' she laughed back at him, knowing that having brought her in on the bus unless he received a message to the contrary he would delay his return until she did come.

Down at the pier Katac made her way over the sloping, weed-slimy jetty to the waiting ferry boat. Already the sea was spread with light though the land was still grey with the gloom of a laggard dawn through which the craggy hills reflected the polish of the night's rain. The crossing was lumpy; the sea sluicing over the bow every time the boat ploughed into a wave and Katac was glad when at last the ferry bumped and grated against the mainland slip. There was another weed-slimy slip to negotiate before she found herself with her two feet firmly on the tarmac of the road. Two minutes' walk and she was in what always appeared to Katac as a city with its twelve shops, its railway station and its fish pier. It was, she soon realized, a sale day and there seemed to be people everywhere, mostly crofters and shepherds who had come in to

buy animals or to sell them and who stood meanwhile in
little groups beside the road, talking and arguing while
their lean, watchful dogs crouched at their heels.

Katac stood for a few minutes looking at the sparse
display in the window of the chemist's shop and when she
felt calm enough to go inside she made her purchases.
Louse powder for the cattle; horse drench; foot rot ointment for the sheep and indigestion powder for her father.
At the Marine store she got coir yarn for tying the hay-
stacks; a new calf pail; a netting needle for her Uncle
Padruig and a pair of rowlocks for her father's dinghy.
Next she called at the bakery where she bought a bag of
fresh cookies and some of the teabread her mother so
much liked. Finally at the General Store after she had
purchased needles and pins and writing paper and
envelopes and all the other odds and ends which never
seemed important until you ran out of them her shopping
list was complete. Complete except for the most important
item of them all, her new boots which she had purposely
left until last.

The lazy bell clanged noisily as she opened and shut the
door of the little dark shop which smelled so strongly of
new leather, Donald's pipe and Donald's dinner. There
came a shuffling noise and Old Donald himself appeared
from a doorway at the back of the shop. He peered at her
for a moment or two and then, 'Why, Katac! It's yourself!' he exclaimed. (Old Donald was past eighty, knew
everybody and never took long to recognize a face.)
'Come away in, lassie.' As he shook her hand he called
over his shoulder towards the doorway from which he
had emerged. 'Bella, see an' get a wee strupak now for
Katac Mackenzie that's here.' Turning to Katac again
he asked, 'Are ye alone the day, lassie?' Concealing her

pride Katac admitted she was. 'My! My!' he said, 'it's growing up fast you are then.' He led her through into a room where a bright coal fire was piled high in the polished range and Bella, Donald's middle-aged daughter was brewing tea. Bella greeted her and setting a chair near the fire told Katac to warm herself. She handed her a cup of steaming tea and on the hob beside her set a plate of cheese sandwiches and another plate of cookies spread with jam. Katac suddenly realized she was hungry and shyly stretching out her hand she helped herself to a sandwich.

Now that the moment had come she felt too shy to mention her new boots and except for replying to Donald's enquiries about her family and the happenings on the island she ate in silence, wishing all the time that Donald would mention the subject of her boots. But he seemed to have forgotten them and when she had drunk two cups of tea and eaten more than half of the sandwiches and cookies he still had not mentioned the reason for her visit. She tried to conceal her mounting dismay as she sat politely while Bella took over the conversation and Donald puffed at his pipe, nodded occasional agreement and spat regularly into the fire. Twice the shop bell clanged and Donald went to answer it. Each time she hoped he would bring her boots when he returned but no! Each time he returned empty handed. Katac was on tenterhooks. Had he forgotten sending the postcard saying her boots had arrived? Or worse, had he in the meantime sold them to someone else? She looked at the clock. Soon she would have to leave to catch the ferry and yet old Donald was just sitting calmly smoking his pipe as if there was all day still to do business. She began to despair. Dare she ask him? she wondered and if she dared how

would she phrase the question obliquely enough to save
them both embarrassment if the boots had already been
sold to someone else? At last with only half an hour to go
before the ferry left she stood up. 'I'd best be on my way,'
she announced.

Donald looked at the clock. 'Aye,' he agreed. 'The
ferry will no be long waitin'.'

Trying to summon up courage to ask about the boots
Katac picked up her bag and pretended to re-arrange her
parcels. Suddenly Donald sat up and knocking out his
pipe emphatically against the bars of the grate said,
'You'll be wantin' your boots, Katac?'

She felt her heart miss a beat. The old bodach, she
thought. He has just been teasing me all the time.

'Aye,' she answered casually, as though she too had only
just remembered them. 'Aye, I may as well take them if
you have them.' She thought her voice sounded tight and
hoped neither Bella nor Donald would notice.

'Didn't I say in the postcard I had them here waitin'
on you?' said Donald testily. 'Sit ye down, lassie, till I get
them.' He went off muttering into the shop and a minute
later returned with a boot box which he dumped on the
table as if it contained something distasteful to him.
Fearful of appearing too eager Katac did not stir for a
moment and then, leaning forward, she slid the box
across the table towards her. She lifted the lid and folded
back a layer of tissue. She caught her breath. The boots
were just as she imagined they would be; black and shiny
and with lovely pointed toes. Her hill boots always had
round stumpy toes which began to turn up after she had
worn them a few times. 'What else can you expect?' her
father had retorted when she had pointed it out to him.
'You're always after goin' uphill in this place an' surely

the toes of your boots will turn up.' Gently Katac lifted the boots from the box; she counted the buttons – eleven on each. Wonderful, she thought. Her mother's best boots had only ten buttons. She wanted to hug them to her but aware that Bella and Donald were watching her she examined the boots critically and allowed her exultation to show only in a small smile of approval. 'They're nice,' she permitted herself to say. Nice indeed! she thought, they're beautiful just!

'Best try them on,' suggested Bella practically.

Katac slipped off her hill boots. Thank goodness she had managed to keep her stockings dry, she reflected as she drew on the new boots. 'They fit fine,' she pronounced.

'Not too tight any place?' questioned Bella.

Katac shook her head. Indeed her toes did feel a wee bitty cramped but she was sure it was only because of the accustomed roominess of her hill boots. 'No,' she insisted firmly, 'they're not too tight at all.' They could have crippled her but she would not have gone away without them now. She slipped them off and put on her hill boots which looked even more clumsy and unsightly than they had before. 'I'll take them,' she told Donald, putting the new boots carefully back into their box.

Donald removed his pipe from his mouth. 'What will you be doin' with boots such as those, lassie?' he demanded scornfully. 'Can ye climb hills and chase after cattle in such things?' he went on. 'Tell me now what is a lassie like you to do with yon?' He pointed the stem of his pipe at the boot box.

Katac smiled and without comment handed him a note from her purse. He took it and still muttering about the unsuitability of the boots he went into the shop and returned with some change. Carefully Katac tucked the boot box at the bottom of her shopping bag and covered it with parcels which would take no harm from a bit of wetting. She thanked Bella for the tea and said goodbye to Old Donald, promising to remember them both to her parents and also to tell her father that Donald had in stock his favourite make of cleated boots.

'You were not forgettin' to come back, then?' Hamish hailed her as he saw her approaching the bus. She climbed in beside him and grinned. 'Did you do all your shoppin'?' he asked.

'Every bit of it,' she told him, indicating her full shopping bags.

On the return trip they collected two male passengers from the hotel where they had been partaking freely of the 'water of life' and for a while the lorry resounded to their vociferous rendering of 'Hello, Patsy Fagan', the two men vying with each other in holding the higher notes but when the first bend in the road abruptly decanted them and the benches on to the pile of mailbags their singing dissolved into a wail of good humoured protest which was itself soon followed by complete silence. Hamish, after stopping the lorry to investigate, reported that they had fallen asleep on the mattress of mailbags.

There were just as many stops on the homeward journey as there had been in the morning but now they were for the depositing of mail in the little pillar boxes. The two merry makers were wakened and put off the bus at their respective gates and a long blast on the horn together with a shout from Hamish ensured that someone would see they reached home safely.

Back home, Katac's mother was waiting at the landing place, a hurricane lantern swinging from her hand. She picked up the bag and with a 'goodnight' to Angus Mhor they went into the cottage. Katac set out her purchases while her mother nodded approval. The new boots she unpacked last of all.

'You'd best get them out of the way before your father sees them just,' her mother said when she saw the box.

Katac nodded. Her father had agreed to her having a pair of light boots but it would not deter him from expressing his scorn when he saw them. She held up the boots for her mother to see and in the lamp light she thought they shone like silk. Her mother's eyes widened and she smiled admiringly as she too counted the buttons. She weighed the boots in her hands. 'My, but they're beautiful just,' she murmured. She handed them back to Katac. 'Beautiful just,' she repeated. Katac was satisfied. Her father would grumble but then she would make sure he did not see the boots until she was wearing them and by then it would be too late to return them.

That night she went to bed rather earlier than usual since not only was she tired after the excitement of her day but she wanted to be alone to admire her boots without being observed. She placed them on top of the clothes chest so she could see them easily from her bed and when she had undressed and said her prayers she lay in her bed watching the flickering candlelight play on her boots. She saw herself taking her place in church the following Sunday and pictured the admiring glances of the other girls most of whom would be wearing their heavy hill boots. Just as she was about to dout the candle a disturbing thought struck her. What if it should be raining so heavily on Sunday that the path to the church was little more than a bog? Birthday present or not she knew in that case she would not be allowed to wear her new boots. The thought was unbearable. Surely it wouldn't rain on Sunday? Surely it couldn't rain and spoil what was to be her special day? She took a deep resolute breath and slipping out of bed she went down on her knees and a little guiltily, a little defiantly, since she had been taught that one does not ask God for personal favours, 'Dear God,' she prayed, 'please, please make it a nice day on Sunday. I do want to wear my shiny boots.'

# A Gun for Sale

The hen that had been sitting on a clutch of eggs for the past three weeks had succeeded in hatching out only three chicks one of which was such a weakling it seemed unlikely to survive.

'An' the other two are cockerels, I doubt,' said Erchy with ill-concealed satisfaction.

'I don't seem to have much success with chick rearing,' I lamented. 'I can't think what I do wrong.'

Erchy looked at me curiously. 'It's more like the cockerel that does wrong,' he quipped.

'Ach, 'tis maybe nothin' to do with you at all,' comforted Morag. 'I mind myself at times havin' trouble with clockin' hens. They're like as though they don't care sometimes whether or no any chicks comes out of the eggs so long as they get a good sit first.'

'Did you keep her quiet while she was clockin'?' probed Erchy. I nodded. 'An' she didn't go leavin' them to get cold?'

'I'm sure she didn't,' I told him.

He shook his head. 'Ach, then I don't know what's the matter with them,' he said and turned his attention to the netting needle which he was dexterously threading in and out through the mesh of a net which looked too dry ever to have seen the sea.

'An' are you sure the cockerel was with the hens before you put down the eggs?' asked Morag.

'Of course he was,' I replied. 'He's always with them.'

'You'd best not be too sure about that,' she warned. 'I mind havin' two sittin's of eggs wasted one after the other an' what did I find was at the back of it but the cockerel had gone off into a sulk because of our own Hector.'

'Because of Hector?' I repeated, biting back a smile.

'Indeed it was so,' she replied with complete seriousness. 'Hector was mendin' a net at the time the way Erchy is doin' now an' I don't rightly know the cause of it but when Hector mends nets it seems he gets kind of tormented into singin' to himself, an' the Dear knows but when Hector sings the cockerel is after leggin' it away that fast the hens don't see him again for maybe more than a day or two.'

I grinned. 'That probably explains it,' I said. 'Hector was doing a bit of net mending down on the shore a few weeks ago. Maybe my cockerel heard him singing and ran for his life.'

'I wouldn't be surprised at that,' said Morag.

'What are you wantin' more chickens for, anyway?' asked Erchy. 'Didn't I see you feedin' your hens on their own eggs not so long back?'

'Yes, I was,' I admitted. 'But you know yourself there is a glut just now.' It seemed stupid to be feeding eggs back to the hens which had laid them but in spring and for most of the summer there were always plenty of eggs and as the number I could myself dispose of was limited and everyone else in Bruach was similarly glutted virtually the only thing left for one to do was to 'put the surplus back where they came from'. At one time I used to pack them into sturdy boxes and post them to friends in England but it seemed to me that either the egg boxes became less sturdy or the post office grew more careless in its handling of them but there came so many reports of broken eggs being received that I gave up the practice. In autumn and winter, however, it was a different story. The autumn moult put a temporary stop to egg production and then, just when the hens had re-feathered and had recommenced laying the winter storms would come to act like a cork on the flow of eggs. Of course in times of plenty I preserved eggs by various methods and these eggs I used for cooking but I missed not being able to indulge a fancy for a fresh egg whenever I felt like it and since in winter not only eggs but fish, milk and crowdie were also scarce and there was the added risk of severe weather isolating us from supplies I was anxious to rear some pullets which should commence laying in the late autumn so that there might be a chance of their carrying on until the older hens began again in the early spring. I had tried the same plan the previous year and it had failed. Now once again I was faced with a meagre hatch of three chicks and as Erchy predicted, with my sort of luck, undoubtedly two of them would turn out to be cockerels. I was disgusted with my broody hen, with my cockerel and with my own apparent inability to foresee and provide the conditions a hen needed to produce a full hatch of chicks.

'I suppose no-one has a sitting hen I could borrow so that I can try again?' I asked hopelessly. As I expected my companions shook their heads. 'Do you know of anyone who has chicks for sale?' I enquired.

'Not hereabouts,' said Erchy, 'but there's a place in the paper says he sells chicks. You could try him if you've a mind.'

Erchy brought the paper and I wrote to the farmer concerned; as a consequence it was arranged that I should collect a dozen day-old chicks from him the following week. As soon as I announced my intention of taking the new car I had acquired to the mainland Morag, Erchy and Hector volunteered to fill the remaining three seats. Morag was coming, as she put it, 'to see a new country just'; Erchy wanted to see a man about a gun and Hector as always wanted to 'see a boat over tsere just'. I sometimes suspected that if I had announced I was proposing to climb Everest Hector would have suggested coming along 'to see a boat over tsere just'.

It was a pleasant day for our journey; calm and mild with rags of mist in the hills and a hazy sun tinting the sea, and as I drove along it struck me, not by any means for the first time, how fortunate I and my companions were that our way of life permitted us to take a few hours off from our work without having to ask permission from an employer or without having a sneaking feeling of guilt that we might be neglecting our chores. Morag of course had Behag to carry on in her absence; Erchy was more or less a freelance and Hector had never at any time succumbed to the burden of regular duties but I, being alone, had got up early and milked my cow and fed the poultry. There had been no mucking out to do since at this time of year Bonny was out on the hill day and night and so until the time came for the evening feeding and milking there was really nothing that demanded my presence. Had I stayed at home I would have been weeding potatoes or stacking peats but so long as the weather did not betray me too badly those tasks would still be accomplished by my working twice as long another day. Meantime I was free; I had amiable company and the car was running sweetly. The auguries were all for a blissful day.

Erchy said, 'If you turn off to the left just down this road we'll come to the place where the fellow lives that has the gun.' I turned off to the left and drove for some miles along a track that snaked around the hill until it finally ended at a drab, peat-stained croft house which squatted beside the loch. Erchy and Hector got out of the car and strolled with apparent aimlessness towards the cottage and, watching, Morag and I saw a bent, cob-webby looking old man emerge, greet them with traditional Highland warmth and lead them into the house. I knew there would soon follow an invitation to Morag and me to go inside and take a 'strupak' but the day was too tempting to stay indoors and I decided on escape. I slung my binoculars round my neck and got out of the car.

'I'm going for a walk,' I told Morag. 'Blow the horn if they're back before I am.'

'Indeed then you might just as well expect to hear the last trumpet as that horn,' she said prophetically. 'I'm thinkin' once them men gets talkin' guns they'll not rouse themselves till one of us puts a rope on them.'

I had made my escape just in time for I was barely out of earshot before I saw the old man approach the car and saw Morag accompany him back to the cottage. I picked my way along the shore until I was well out of sight and then I sat down on a lichened boulder at the edge of the water, savouring the still reflections and the near silence of the hill-guarded loch. In Bruach the water was almost always too shaggy for reflections and invariably there was a noise of sea, whether it was the violence of storms, the snarling surge of after-storm swell or simply the sucking and hissing of the tide. It was a change for me to rest beside quiet water for though this was a sea-loch the entrance was a narrow channel between opposing head-lands so that, save in stormy weather, it was sheltered and still, the wavelets chiming against the shingle with a sound like the tinkle of draught-stirred baubles on a Christmas tree. I focussed my glasses on a thin crust of black rocks which reached out into the water about half way up the loch, intrigued by the pattern made by the quiescent gulls which had ranged themselves with such precision against their black background that the effect was of a piano keyboard. The loch itself was stippled with seabirds: mergansers, razorbills and shelduck. Drifts of eiders paddled around the margins voicing their prim-voiced exclamations; flights of oystercatchers rose to skim across the water as they shrieked their wild alarms while close at hand rock pipits flitted busily over the shallows. As always the beauty of it all filled me with humility while at the same time making me fearful of its desecration and I found myself murmuring my favourite lines from 'Inversnaid' and murmuring them with all the fervency of a prayer:

> *'What would the world be once bereft*
> *Of wet and of wilderness? Let them be left,*
> *O let them be left, wildness and wet;*
> *Long live the weeds and the wilderness yet.'*

I stood up. I had suggested to Erchy that an hour was a reasonable time for him to conclude negotiations about the gun and after an extra half hour to allow for the crofters' indifference to clock time I started back towards the car. There was no sign of them so I sat down once again to admire the scenery while keeping a sharp eye on the cottage since I knew that if, when they came out to reconnoitre, I was not visible, they would simply go back into the house to continue drinking tea and gossiping until I made my presence felt. After another half hour of waiting I began to grow impatient. The purpose of my journey had after all been for me to collect my chickens and naturally I wanted to ensure that I did eventually reach the farmer's house before it was time to start on the homeward journey. Apart from blowing the horn which would not only have been a breach of Highland courtesy but would have been a blasphemy in such surroundings I wondered how I could attract the attention of my companions without going to the house and so risk having to stay for a 'strupak'. I suddenly recalled Hector's method of attracting my attention when he was too shy to come near the house such as when I had guests staying with me. He simply used to take off his cap and fling it at the hens, scattering them in panic. The resulting cacophony would bring me hurrying to the door prepared to do battle with a maurauding dog or a flock of thieving hoody crows and usually I would be just in time to see Hector adjusting his hat on his head with all the aplomb of just having raised it in salutation while he stared at the hens with well simulated surprise. I never divulged that I was aware of the strategy but since it proved unfailingly effective I resolved to try it now. I was not wearing any sort of head covering but there was a small cushion in the car which I always used to support my back when driving and thinking it would make an excellent substitute I resolved to throw that. At the precise instant the cushion left my hand I glimpsed out of the corner of my eye the old man appearing round the gable end of the cottage. He was followed by Erchy, Hector and Morag and their varying expressions as they caught me in the act of hurling the cushion imprinted themselves on my memory. Erchy looked plainly startled. Hector contrived to look exaggeratedly indifferent and Morag and the old man stared at me with that strangely hunted look which, had they been devout papists, would have been accompanied by the precaution of crossing themselves. To make things worse the sudden appearance of the old man had caused me to misjudge my aim and though the hens scattered and squawked with an embarrassing clamour alas! my cushion landed in a battered tin bath half full of sludgy water. I knew how inexplicably crazy my action must have looked and found myself shaking with inward laughter as I hastily retrieved the cushion. I knew too that at least in front of the old man I must restrain my mirth and sensing that it was wiser to proffer no excuse for my conduct I merely smiled fatuously. Morag spoke in Gaelic and the old man's expression changed to one of happy understanding. Erchy soured his mouth to disguise a smile and Hector gazed with serious concentration at the smoking chimney of the cottage. I guessed she had given her own highly individual explanation of my action and wondered what it might be.

# *Bait!*

'Now, are we ready to carry on,' I said after successfully resisting the old man's pressing invitation to take a strupak.

'Aye,' Erchy nodded. Morag got into the car and promptly took on to her lap a stone firkin jar which, I heard her promising the old man, she would leave at the post office to be filled with paraffin ready for the postman to bring out next time he came with mail. Erchy got in cherishing a twelve-bore hammer shotgun which looked to me as if it might have done duty at Waterloo, and Hector had clutched in his hand a 'tsing' which, after a few puzzled glances, I thought I identified as the speaking tube from an old Rolls-Royce. The articles Hector succeeded in disinterring from old byres never ceased to astonish me. When I took my seat behind the wheel I regretted having even thought of throwing my cushion at the hens for despite its brief immersion it was far too damp now to use and I was compelled to drive without its familiar support behind the small of my back. I was assailed by the feeling that the day which had begun so well was beginning to deteriorate but I shrugged off the thought, dismissing it as probably no more than the first pangs of hunger making themselves felt.

'Can we stop somewhere for a bite to eat?' I proposed when we were back on the main road. 'I'm feeling a bit peckish.'

'Ach, you should have come in an' taken a wee strupak with the old man,' Erchy told me.

'Indeed, mo ghaoil, you'd be best pleased you didn't,' said Morag. 'The room we was in was in such a state you could have stirred it with a stick.'

'I mind there is a hotel we could get somethin',' Erchy recalled. 'It's on a bitty yet but I believe they'd give us a meal if we asked them for it.'

I drove on until Morag, espying the post office, asked me to stop so that she could leave the old man's firkin jar, and remembering that in my coat pocket were two letters I had intended posting at the first opportunity I announced that I would go in and buy some stamps.

'Ach, you shouldn't buy stamps from this place,' Erchy warned.

'Why ever not? It's a post office, isn't it?' I asked.

'Aye, right enough but I was in there once when I came to collect a dog I'd bought an' the old folks that was runnin' the place didn't seem to know a stamp from a telegram,' he explained.

'Had they no had it long then?' enquired Morag.

'Forty years,' said Erchy. 'You'd think they would have learned in that time or else had it taken away from them.'

'If they had it forty years the postmaster maybe hadn't the heart to take it away from them,' suggested Morag.

'Maybe so,' allowed Erchy, 'but judgin' from the stamps they sold to me that day I'd think they'd likely had them in stock for forty years as well. There wasn't a one of them would stick on an envelope.'

I chuckled.

'It's as true as I'm here,' he affirmed. 'An' when I showed the old bodach the way they wouldn't stick he tried would he do it himself an' he brought his fist down with such a bang on the envelope the damty stamp broke into little bits. Honest,' he reiterated, 'he was still pickin' the bits off himself when I left him.'

'In that case I won't post my letters here,' I said. 'But please be sure and remind me as soon as we see another post office. They should have been posted two or three days ago and now they're very urgent.' I have an unfortunate habit of what my friends describe as 'taking my letters for a walk', i.e. I set out with the intention of posting them but something distracts me and on my return home I find the letters still in my pocket or in the pocket of the car.

'I'll try to remember,' promised Erchy.

'Supposin' I forget my own name I'll remind you to post your letters,' Hector swore fervidly.

When Morag returned after depositing the firkin Erchy observed, 'I hate to see those jars bein' used for paraffin. It gives me a kind of queer feelin' inside myself.' He regarded us with a pained expression.

'Why?' I asked.

'When I was young they were always full of whisky, not paraffin, that's why,' he explained. 'All the old folks had at least a firkin of whisky they kept beside the fire ready to warm them when they came in from the cold.'

'Aye, tse old folks always had plenty whisky,' corroborated Hector with a deep sigh of regret.

'An' there's plenty of the old folks would be glad they died when they did sooner than suffer the pain of knowin' the price of whisky today,' added Morag.

My companions relapsed into silence as they no doubt meditated on how pleasant life must have been in the halcyon days when whisky was as easily available as tea is today.

'Did I hear you sayin' you came here to collect a dog one time?' asked Morag after a little while and when Erchy nodded she went on, 'Which dog would that be?'

'The old one I have still,' replied Erchy.

'An' I paid good money for him, I'm tellin' you. I was done over that dog. He was supposed to be well trained.' He snorted. 'He was that well trained when I got him home he didn't know to come for his food when it was put for him.'

'He's a good dog with the sheep, surely?' argued Morag.

'Aye, right enough he's good now for all that he's too
deaf to know what I'm after tellin' him but when I first
got him he didn't know a sheep from a stoat.'

'Dogs don't seem as if tsey take to me,' observed
Hector.

'And you don't take to dogs!' I tossed the accusation
at him. 'You're a menace to any dog.' It was true. Whenever Hector saw a dog he would surreptitiously pick up a
stone and when he had got safely past without being bitten
he would throw the stone from behind him so that even
the owner of the dog was unaware of his action. But the
dogs all knew and welcomed him accordingly.

'Aye, if Hector gets himself a bite it will be himself to
blame,' agreed Morag. Hector's response was a limp
smile.

'Now,' I said, after we had driven a few more miles.
'Let's get the day sorted out, shall we?' I want to collect
my chickens last of all so that they're not confined too long
in the box so if we can find this hotel and get some lunch
we can then go to this place where Hector wants to look
at the boat.'

'Tsat's not so far now,' interrupted Hector.

'And if you don't take too much time over that,' I
continued in a severe tone, 'then we can carry on and
collect my chickens and start for home in good time for
me to be back to milk Bonny and feed the hens.'

'Right enough,' agreed Morag.

I glanced round to get Hector's acceptance and saw
that he was looking intently into the mouthpiece of his
speaking tube; Erchy was staring straight in front of him
and his eyes were impishly bright. Once again the sense
that the day was deteriorating assailed me.

'Here is the hotel I was tellin' you of,' said Erchy and I

turned off the road and pulled in at an austere looking establishment which bore no sign proclaiming it to be a hotel.

'They must have had the sign down for the winter an' not put it back yet,' said Morag. We went inside and settled ourselves in the deserted bar, while Morag went to investigate the nether regions with a view to ordering lunch.

I sniffed. 'Peculiar smell,' I whispered to Erchy.

He sniffed. 'Damty queer, right enough,' he agreed and rapped with his knuckles on the bar counter. There was no response but after a little while we heard footsteps approaching. It was Morag who appeared.

'Indeed but we'll get no lunch here today,' she told us.

'Why not?' I asked despairingly. I was by now very hungry.

'They're sayin' the cook's gone off,' she explained.

'That's what's after makin' yon queer smell,' said Erchy with a wink at me. He rapped again more emphatically on the counter and this time his assault was followed by the sound of footsteps clumping down bare wood stairs. A surly young woman enquired with her eyes what we wanted but when we asked for food, pleading even for a sandwich, she told us brusquely that they were short staffed and were far too busy getting the place ready for the season to be able to offer us anything but drinks and biscuits. I said I would have a dry sherry but when it came it was sweet sherry; only the biscuits were dry.

'Well,' I murmured, 'you certainly can't accuse this place of giving us a Highland welcome.'

Morag was ashamed. 'Indeed it's that crabbit you

would think it must be English folks that's runnin' it,' she said. There were times when Morag completely forgot I was English.

'Ach, what else do you expect from a place that leaves the cook to go off,' said Erchy.

When we came out of the hotel there was a thick mist like grey fleece crouching behind the hills ready to bear down on us and before we had got very far along the road I had to use the windscreen wipers. With the change in the weather and with my stomach complaining of neglect it seemed that my earlier misgivings were already beginning to be justified.

'I hope this boat of yours isn't far away now,' I said to Hector.

'About half a mile just,' he informed me blithely. But being familiar with Hector's estimation of distance I wisely interpreted his 'half a mile just' as probably being nearer three miles. Once again our road skirted the shores of a loch around which were scattered the homes of landless cottars built so close to the water's edge that their washing lines were stretched above the shingle between the margin of the tides so that it must have been possible to peg out or take in washing only when the tide was sufficiently low. As we turned away from the loch the cottars' houses and the crofts gave way to efficient looking farms and everywhere we looked we saw that the crops were far more advanced than those in Bruach. Already their potatoes grew in stately rows whereas in Bruach they were still only squat posies above the earth; the fields of corn were bristly green whereas in Bruach the green was barely more than a portent; the fields set aside for hay were lush with silky grass while our grass had not yet grown high enough to camouflage the hoofprints of the cattle which had fought and grazed over the crofts all winter.

'They're well on with the crops,' observed Erchy, voicing all our thoughts.

'They're always well on in these sort of places,' asserted Morag knowledgeably. 'They get their spring work done early an' then at the back end when we're still gatherin' in the corn these folks is away on their holidays an' all their harvest finished.'

'They probably have plenty of help,' I pointed out.

'Is it help?' exclaimed Morag. 'Indeed when I was away on my tour we was one day at a farm where they had what they said was a concubine harvester an' the farmer was after tellin' me it did everythin' for him just; not just cuttin' the corn but threshin' it an balin' the straw.'

'We could do with one of those in Bruach,' said Erchy.

'An' what would we do in Bruach with a concubine harvester?' demanded Morag. 'The men wouldn't know how to behave with it just.'

'They'd soon find out,' I assured her.

We were approaching a crossroads and Hector asked me to turn right and then drive in through a gap in a stone wall which bounded a field adjoining a prosperous looking croft house.

'Is this it?'

'Aye,' he said, getting out of the car. 'Are you comin'?' he asked Erchy. Erchy followed him and they disappeared from sight behind some buildings.

'It doesn't look a very boaty sort of place,' I said to Morag. We both got out of the car and had embarked on an inspection of the land when a middle-aged woman appeared and with real Highland cordiality invited us to take a 'strupak'. In her aseptically clean kitchen we drank mugs of strong tea and ate wads of soggy Glasgow bread spread with home-made butter and thin factory-made jam that dribbled anaemically between our fingers while we ate. With my hunger appeased we went outside again but just as I was beginning to think the day had improved I caught sight of Erchy and Hector struggling to load a large barrel on to the back seat of the car.

'What's this?' I demanded in outrage.

'Aye, well, d'you see,' began Hector nimbly. ' 'Tis my creels. I have no bait for tsem.'

'You're not telling me that barrel is full of bad fish?' I expostulated.

'No full,' he disclaimed. 'No more than half, just.'

I opened the door of the car and the smell made me reel back. 'I'm not driving all the way back to Bruach with that appalling stink in the car,' I told him emphatically.

'It is too big to go into tse boot,' Hector explained. 'Anyway, it will no be so bad once we get goin',' he hastened to assure me. 'Wis tse windows open we'll likely not notice tse smell, I doubt.'

'I am not taking that barrel back to Bruach,' I said firmly. 'You'll have to take it out.'

He turned and scratched away under his cap. 'Indeed I don't know how will we get it out wisout spillin' it,' he mumbled. 'It was bad enough gettin' it in just but if we have to take it out again I believe it will spill for sure.' I believed that too and my moment of hesitation gave him his chance to plead further. 'An' see I cannot get bait anywhere at all and tsere's creels lyin' on tse shore for want of it an' tse lobsters waitin' tsere in tse sea to be caught.'

'You're breaking my heart,' I snapped. It was by no

means the first time Hector had played such a confidence trick on me. 'What about the boat you came to see?' I taxed him.

He scuffed his boot on the ground. 'Aye, well, tsey must have sold it a while back,' he disclosed in a chastened mutter.

'Hector!' I upbraided him furiously. 'You really are a bounder. You knew perfectly well there was no boat for you to see and you knew perfectly well if you'd mentioned one word to me about coming to buy lobster bait you would have been left behind in Bruach.'

His eyes widened guilelessly. 'I didn't buy it,' he denied. 'Tsey wouldn't take anytsing for it.' I blinked. If they wouldn't take anything for it then I reckoned the bait must be really putrid. Hector brightened, assuming the fact that he had got something for nothing would help me to accept the situation more easily. 'Tsey had it since a whiley now y'see, an' tsey were sayin' it's after losin' some of it's liquor so tsey're wantin' rid of it.'

'It smells to me as if they've kept it for years,' I remarked bitterly.

'Three, anyway,' supplied Erchy.

I knew I was beaten since if I insisted on the bait being taken out of the car then Hector and possibly Erchy too would see to it that a good deal more of the liquor would be lost and most of it would be lost inside my car. The resulting graveolence would, I knew, linger for months afterwards. For me the day finally dissolved into wretchedness. I flopped angrily into my seat. There was no room now for Erchy in the back of the car and he had to sit at the front and nurse Morag on his knee which meant that I too was cramped. With Morag's elbow in my shoulder and without my cushion for support my driving position was exceedingly uncomfortable and as I drove through the mist and rain to the farm where I was to collect my chickens I cursed Hector and all his works. Fortunately there was no hitch with the chickens. I handed the box to Hector.

'Look after those for me,' I commanded. 'And don't you dare open the lid for fear they'll be overcome by fumes.'

Nauseated by the smell of the rotting bait and seething over Hector's duplicity I kept my jaws clenched and my foot as well down on the accelerator as I dared. Hector was not a nice man, I told myself firmly, and from henceforth I must cease to regard him as the rather lovable rogue whose faults I had always found so easy to condone. He was all rogue; a laggard; a Lothario and a liar and I must ensure that never again would he be given the chance to involve me in any of his schemes.

Back in Bruach Behag came to watch us unload.

'So you got your bait,' she complimented her husband, thus dispelling any lingering doubt that the purpose of Hector's journey had been the collection of the bait. 'But what have you there?' she went on, as she saw Hector swinging the speaking tube.

'Ach, 'tis for Erchy to put in his dog's ear,' he told her. 'He's always girnin' the beast's that deaf he doesn't know what he's sayin'.' He gave it to her to hold while he and Erchy struggled to get the barrel out of the car which mercifully they did without spilling it.

'Ach, I don't know how to tell you how pleased I am to get it,' he said with fervent apology.

'And I don't know how to tell you how pleased I am to get rid of it,' I mimicked acridly.

He raised his voice. 'Miss Peckwitt's to get tse first

lobster tsat gets into tse creel,' he promised but seeing no change in the frigidity of my expression he became even more generous. 'Not tse first one but tse first tree she shall have,' he vowed, holding up three fingers by way of emphasis.

'I'll bloody well deserve them!' I retorted savagely. None of them had heard me use such an epithet before and their startled expressions made me burst into laughter which Hector instantly interpreted as forgiveness. He stretched his lips into his version of a smile and his wide blue eyes glowed with touching affection.

I let in the clutch but just as the car began to move I remembered something and, braking, I called to Morag. 'Morag, what did you say to that old man when you came out and caught me in the act of hurling the cushion at his hens?' I asked her.

She sucked in a smile. 'Indeed, mo ghaoil, didn't I tell him you were after wantin' a sittin' hen an' you would be throwin' the cushion thinkin' maybe one of his hens would sit on it,' she told me.

I grinned. 'I expect he thinks I'm completely mad,' I said.

'Ach,' she demurred but without conviction.

The removal of the barrel of bait had not removed the smell from the car and deciding that a damp interior was preferable to a smelly one I left the doors and windows open while I milked Bonny, fed the hens and transferred my new chickens from their box to the hay-lined brooder I had made for them. The chicks appeared healthy enough, I thought, so at least, despite tribulations, the day had not been a complete fiasco. It was not until I went out later to close up the car for the night that I noticed my unposted letters still in the pocket.

## The Highlander

She stood alone on the highest of the hill paths, silhouetted against the bloated grey sky and with the brisk, ice-edged wind rippling through the shaggy hair of her coat. The rest of the herd moved on steadily grazing its way down towards the glen and paying no attention to the straggler who, minute by minute, was being left further and further behind. Her yearning eyes followed the progress of her former companions and she lifted her head with its wide sweep of horns to give a loud moo of protest at their desertion. Her fuzzy ears twitched uncomprehendingly as the herd ignored her and her black ringed muzzle – birthmark of the true bred Highland cow – sniffed anxiously. She knew a moment of panic as she perceived how great had become the distance between her and the other cattle and lumbered a few indecisive steps after them, torn between the desire to gallop down the hill to join them and the strange impulse which all morning had been urging her to detach herself from the herd. After one last glance at the receding cows she turned and with steady deliberation plodded back the way she had come.

She had covered about half a mile before she paused, but this time her glance was not in the direction the herd had taken but was one of appraisal of a sheltered hollow in the side of the hill hugged by a crooked outcrop of rocks and fringed by a few stunted and leafless hazels. Quickening her gait she made towards it, the wind frisking her long tail against her legs like a gentle goad. When she reached the hollow she inspected it with restless curiosity but though she found grass there that was as yet unravaged by the winter storms and though she had eaten little since the previous evening her tongue did not curl out to snatch it into her mouth. Instead after several minutes of contemplation she lay down with a small grunt of discomfort and tried unsuccessfully to bring up her cud. A vanguard of snowflakes swirled experimentally into the hollow, stippling the short moor grass around her; settling easily on her coat and melting as they slid over her wide eyes. Slowly the twisted shapes of the hazels became outlined in white and the wind resolved itself into a steady sibilance.

With the first stab of pain she heaved herself to her feet, her ears twitching; her tail held out stiffly and when the pain had eased she still stood tensely, lifting her hind leg every now and then in an attempt to kick away whatever it was that was biting at her belly. At the second stab she began to pant and her eyes grew wider, showing the whites around the pupils. She was afraid now and yet despite her fear there was an instinctive acceptance of the pain as being a function of her destiny; the culmination of a sequence of events which had begun with the increasing heaviness of her belly; her desire to seek for certain herbs among the grass; her unease of the morning and the compulsion to get away from the rest of the herd.

As the pain again left her she lay down giving a plaintive gasp as her swollen body touched the ground. Almost immediately the pain returned, convulsing her belly and, agitated by its intensity she half rose but the pain was swifter and shorter than the earlier ones and she sagged down before she was fully on her feet. The spasms now followed quickly, one after another, boring through her body and between each spasm she rested her head on the ground while her steamy breath escaped with heavy whimperings from her nostrils. She became aware that under her tail there was movement and she wanted to turn herself round to discover what it was but she was no longer in control of her own impulses; the pain was in complete possession of her body and she could only strain desperately trying to rid herself of its grip while snatching at moments of respite to gather strength for the next spasm. Suddenly she lifted her head and gave a sharp, short bellow that was compounded of pain and fear. She tried vainly to struggle to her feet; her body contracted violently once, twice, thrice and as the third contraction rid her of the pain she heard a stifled nicker. Turning her head to investigate she saw the tiny, wet, brown body of her calf struggling on the snowy ground. Her eyes dilated with wonder and alarm; her body throbbed with compassion and then, swamped by a flood of mother love she rose quickly to her feet and turning herself round began to croon and lick at him with gentle urgency. As the calf tried to rise she licked the slime from his tight-curled coat with her rough tongue and when he managed shakily to gain his feet she nuzzled him towards the warmth and shelter of her body quivering with joy when she felt the firm little head pushing against her belly and the wet explorative muzzle bunting excitedly at her distended udder. Her body relaxed as his mouth eventually closed on one of her teats and he began to suck, weakly at first and then with increasing purpose while his small tail swung ecstatically as the thick, warm colostrum trickled down his gullet. Carefully the cow shifted herself to a more comfortable position and as her long-lashed lids drooped over eyes that were opaque with the rapture of motherhood she brought up her cud and chewed contentedly.

The calf continued to suck, sheltered by her body from the cold wind and the thickening snow and when he was replete he collapsed on the ground. With worried croonings she nudged him up on to his tottery feet and towards the shelter of a rock where, with her hoof, she scraped the snow from a patch of coarse grass. Understanding her action the calf lay down and, tucking his head into his flank, he slept while his mother horned away the snow from sedge and heather clumps and blew upon it with her warm breath before she began to graze. When the after-birth came she ate it instinctively, licking the grass where it had been to obliterate any trace of smell that might attract a roaming fox and as evening showed greyly through the still falling snow she lay down beside her calf, positioning her head so that it was a roof protecting him from the blizzard.

At the first hint of dawn she roused him with the diligence of her attentions and encouraged him once again to relieve the heaviness of her udder. He was sturdier now and found the teats without difficulty and when at last he was satisfied instead of lying down he kicked up his back legs and almost fell in the attempt to express his delight. The cow moved forward three or four steps and lowed to him to follow. The calf lurched after her and rubbed himself against her flank. She moved forward again still calling to him persuasively and as he gambolled after her, his shaky legs gaining strength with every step, he answered her with thin pules of complaint.

The blizzard had ceased with the dawn; the wind had dropped to a wavering breeze and the emerging sun flushed the whitened moors. The cow began slowly climbing back towards the path where she had parted from her companions the previous day, stopping frequently to give a reassuring and proprietory lick at her calf. When she reached the path she stood and gave a loud enquiring bellow that the bare hills echoed and the snow blanketed moors absorbed. She listened intently and as if in response bellowed again, assertively. Raising her muzzle she sniffed into the breeze and as the scent of the herd reached her she gave a further bellow that was unmistakeably triumphant. Resolutely she made towards the glen, the fresh snow compacting beneath her hooves, her calf trotting confidently by her side.

In a very short time now she and her calf would be joining the herd.

# Tizzie

As I threw out the water after having washed up my tea things I saw Old Alistair coming to the cottage. 'He Breeah!' I called in answer to his greeting and going inside I took a bottle of nettle beer and a glass from the larder and stood by the door waiting for him. Except for Janet's house where he was to be found most evenings waiting his turn to read the paper and also holding forth at the subsequent ceilidh Alistair rarely bothered to visit any of his neighbours but in summer he sometimes made an excuse to call on me to drink a glass or two of my nettle beer. He was a vociferous traditionalist constantly proclaiming the industriousness of the women of his mother's generation while affecting to despise the present-day women of Bruach because they no longer devoted themselves to such time-honoured occupations as spinning and weaving and dyeing wool; grinding their own oatmeal between the quern stones and preparing medicines and ointments from the wild plants and herbs which were to be found on the moors. They were 'spoiled with the vans' he was frequently heard to declare.

Alistair's own mother, he was fond of telling me, had regularly made not nettle beer but nettle tea for her family and he claimed that this annual 'nettle scourin' ' as he called it kept both adults and children healthy for the rest of the year. When I suggested he should make his own nettle tea he looked at me askance. It was not a man's place to do such things, he informed me though being a bachelor he regularly cooked and cleaned for himself.

Whenever Alistair came he was always careful to bring as recompense for the beer some small gift which he thought might interest me: a fossil ammonite; a hollowed out tonka bean; an unusual pipe fish which he had caught and which, because of its hard, scaly skin, had in drying out retained its living shape were some of the things he bestowed on me and which were added to my collection. He was always careful too to come on a nice day so that he could insist on drinking his beer outside for despite his tendency to rant he was a shy man and since his traditionalism led him to deplore the efforts I had made to modernize my cottage he preferred to stay outside rather than feel himself constrained to express his contempt for them too strongly. He had already informed me he did not like the new windows which had been installed, maintaining that they were 'misliked by the walls' and when he saw my new cooking stove for the first time he denounced it grouchily as looking as out of place in a croft kitchen as a giraffe would look in a cow byre, a comment which when I retailed it to Morag brought the response: 'Ach, that man is so far back he cannot even taste a cake that has been baked in an oven.'

I untied the string from round the neck of the bottle and eased out the cork; the beer foamed over the glass as I handed it to Alistair who eyed it approvingly and as he took the glass in his right hand he thrust in front of me the spread palm of his left hand on which reposed three tiny creagags which he had caught while fishing off the rocks. Large creagags were greatly enjoyed by the Bruachites but I found them glutinous and bony; the small ones were usually thrown back into the sea as being useless for anything but when I saw the fish Alistair offered I exclaimed with delight.

'No wonder Tizzie is excited,' I told him.

Tizzie had joined me one day in early summer when, having been too plagued by the midges to continue working on the croft and having been too loath to spend such a warm day indoors, I had in desperation taken my boat and rowed out until I was far enough away from the shore to escape the attentions of the midges. It was sultry on the land and so calm on the sea that when I rested on my oars the drips from the blades were the only discernible ruffle on the surface of the water and after rowing aimlessly for some time I shipped the oars and allowing the boat to drift with the tide I rejoiced in the coolness and the ever absorbing pastime of peering down into the green depths. Shifting my position after a time to the other side of the boat I glanced up to see a black-back gull swooping repeatedly at something on the sea well astern of the boat but it was a minute or two before I could make out the tiny, panic-stricken baby guillemot which was paddling frantically as it tried to escape the gull's attack. Every time the gull swooped for the kill the chick dived but the time it could remain submerged was limited and as it bobbed to the surface the enemy came again, the cruel beak ready to snatch and shake the life out of its victim before tearing out its entrails. The black-back's manoeuvres were unhurried. The chick would soon tire and the gull had only to continue swooping until the guillemot was too exhausted to dive and then he would merely have to lift his prey from the water.

I grabbed my oars and rowed to the rescue and surprisingly when the chick saw the boat approaching instead of diving or paddling away in fright it came purposefully towards it, cheeping imploringly. As I shipped an oar and put my hand into the water like a scoop the guillemot swam into it with complete trust to crouch like a small black ball of fluff on my palm. Immediately it ceased its cheeping and I held the chick to my breast as the shadow of the black-back's wings swept close over us. Back the black-back came again so close his beak was within inches of the gunwale. I put the chick safely under a thwart where it stayed quiet and still while the black-back, cheated of its prey, squawked its fury and flew away. The chick closed its eyes.

While I rowed about the sea hoping to find a distracted parent or indeed any other guillemots near which I could safely leave the chick it slept beneath the thwart and I was astounded and moved by its apparent trust in me. For more than an hour I rowed without seeing so much as a feather of another guillemot and since I had to return home and carry on with the work I had left I scanned the sky for the presence of black-backs. Satisfied there were none in the vicinity I lifted the chick and put it gently back into the sea whereat it squeaked protestingly and refused to swim away from the boat. I started to row but the chick followed, its little webbed feet paddling desperately after the boat and its squeaking becoming so full of entreaty that I was compelled to stop and let it catch up again. It was such a defenceless little thing that I wanted more than anything to take it home with me but, I told myself firmly, it was too ridiculous to think of hand-rearing a baby guillemot. The sea was its true home and despite the hazards it would stand more chance of surviving there than it would stand with me. I rowed on, but the guillemot refused to be left behind and after one or two more attempts to elude it I yielded and lifted it into the boat. Back again under the protection of the thwart the chick dozed contentedly.

On the shore I put it at the edge of the tide hoping it would swim away from the land but as I moved it followed me closely pecking at my shoes so I carried it back to the cottage and fed it with slivers of fish cut from a fillet I had been intending to cook for my own supper. It ate them greedily before recommencing its monotony of squeaks which were like those of a stuffed toy. I made a bed for it in a cardboard box lined with an old pyjama jacket and it accepted the nest unhesitatingly, fluffing out its feathers as it settled down among the folds of cloth.

Since I was not certain the bird was a guillemot I got

out my bird book which seemed to confirm that it might be and later I asked some of my neighbours if they could identify it. They told me the Gaelic name for it but since I could not find the name in my Gaelic dictionary I was not much enlightened.

'Ach, I believe they have some other name for it as well in some parts,' Morag told me, shaking her head. 'But I cannot bring it to mind though indeed it is teasin' at me like the drip on the end of my nose.'

'Would it be a tystie?' I asked. My bird book said that black guillemots were called tysties in the Orkney Islands.

'Indeed that is the very word,' confirmed Morag. And so I called the chick 'Tystie' which quickly became 'Tizzie' because it was easier to call 'Tizzie' than 'Tystie'. In no time at all Tizzie learned to answer to her name. She learned also to associate seaboots with the proffering of fish and even when she was in her box and covered up to quell her interminable squeaking it needed only the sound of boots clumping outside to start the pyjama jacket agitating and a moment or two later Tizzie would launch herself over the side of the box and on to the floor where she would rush to peck at the boots in the certainty they were bringing fresh fish for her.

She began to dominate my life. I found myself hauling up pails of sea water to fill an old zinc bath which she could use as a swimming pool; I begged fish; I spent hours fishing from the rocks which was by no means one of my favourite occupations and when the weather was too rough for any other sort of fishing I searched the rock pools and the shore for small crabs and catfish all of which she swallowed with hungry indifference and when replete she slept quietly and snugly in her box.

When she had been with me six weeks Tizzie was taking up to a whole mackerel or its equivalent in twelve hours and though in summer fish was not too difficult to procure I did not know how I would cope during the winter when it was virtually unobtainable and when the period of daylight was too short to cram in all the work of the croft without having the added burden of seeking for crabs and catfish even if the weather allowed access to the shore. But I knew I would have to find some way of providing for her even if it meant sending to the mainland for a few months' supply of tinned sardines.

As Tizzie matured her colouring changed to snowy white in front and dark grey to almost black on her back and her posture as she approached a human – which she did completely without fear – was so upright that tourists seeing her would exclaim 'Oh, look! A baby penguin!' Whenever I could spare the time I took her down to the sea and waited while she bobbed about in the water and despite my attachment to her I hoped for her own sake the day would come when she would feel the call of the wild and return to her own kind. But Tizzie appeared to have no instinct whatsoever to return to her natural environment and the fact worried me.

I was even more worried when I received an invitation to my nephew's wedding which was to take place in England. It was an invitation which I knew I must accept and I wondered what was to happen to Tizzie whilst I was away. I certainly could not take a guillemot to a wedding nor could I expect my neighbours to give up time to look after her particularly as the haymaking season was in full swing. Erchy and Hector gallantly offered to share the task of feeding her and Morag promised to keep an eye on her until I returned but despite their assurances I doubted if they would be able to look after her as well as I had done. I knew they would do their best but just at that time I was anxious about an increasing lethargy I had noticed in Tizzie; a certain droopiness about the wings and I was full of foreboding.

When I returned from the wedding I knew from Erchy's face that Tizzie was dead. 'We fed her all right,' he explained. 'But she didn't seem as if she wanted her food after a day or two an' when we put her into the sea she was like as if she couldn't swim at all.'

'I had a feeling she was sickening when I went away,' I acknowledged. 'I was wondering if she hadn't enough oil in her feathers through being so much on land.'

'More likely you overfed her just,' suggested Erchy.

'Maybe,' I said.

'Aye well it could be this is the best way for it to happen,' he said. 'An' it was a better death than the beast would have known if that black-back had got her.'

'I suppose it was,' I admitted. But it was small comfort.

# Sucky

'Four o'clock in the mornin', mind,' said Erchy.

'Four o'clock,' I repeated. 'I'll be ready.'

'An' see you have a good stick,' he called after me.

Twice a year, once in the spring and once in the autumn a cattle sale was held in a village some fourteen miles from Bruach and it was a tradition that those crofters who were disposing of beasts should combine for the droving. The sale was always timed to start at nine o'clock and it was necessary to walk the cattle through half the night so as to be at the field in time for them to have a brief rest and a feed before the auctioneer arrived and the proceedings commenced. This autumn I myself had a beast to sell and I had been to call on Erchy to confirm the time for the start of the droving. There was no need for me to attend the cattle sale. Erchy or one of the other crofters would willingly have taken charge and done all that was needed to be done but I had elected to accompany them partly because though I had participated in almost every other activity in Bruach I had never before joined in the droving of cattle through the night and partly because I was proud of the beast I had reared and wanted to see for myself how he compared with others at the sale.

He was Bonny's first calf and I called him 'Sucky', and almost from the hour of his birth we had been rivals for our share of his mother's milk. In Bruach there were three methods of calf rearing. You could leave the calf 'at foot' which meant that you allowed it to remain with its mother and suckle all the milk; or you could take it away at birth, milk the cow yourself and feed the calf its share from a pail or you could compromise, as I had done with Sucky, letting him have a half share of his mother so that he sucked two teats while I milked the other two. It was not, I found, a particularly satisfactory arrangement because not only did Sucky bunt frequently thus knocking the milk-slippery teats and often the pail from my grasp but Bonny seemed able to control the direction of the milk flow so that he got at least twice as much milk from the two teats allocated to him as I got from the other two no matter how careful I was to milk alternate pairs of teats. But once Bonny was back again on the hill and enjoying the company of the other cattle and feeding on the young heather shoots she became less eager to return to her calf for the twice daily suckling and thus more inclined to let down her milk for me. So, like the other crofters, I was soon making the twice daily journey to the moors to milk her and, after keeping back enough for my own needs I fed the rest to Sucky from a pail. Although I told myself firmly that because he was a bull calf I must not allow myself more than an expedient affection for him I loved feeding 'Sucky': the smell of the warm milk; the bawled greetings as I appeared with the pail; the cavorting about the pen; the excitedly thrashing tail; the blue eyes rolling with anticipatory greed; the feel of his rough tongue on my fingers as I guided his muzzle down into the pail and the sensuous half closed eyes as he felt the warm milk trickling into his belly. Even when the pail was empty his sucking mouth still sought my fingers and when, for the sake of his digestion, I eventually withdrew them he made little grunts of protest as he realized that his meal was finished. After a couple of weeks he no longer needed my fingers to suck and he would dive his head into the pail the moment I got near enough for him to reach it. While he drank the milk and then with his abrasive tongue licked the pail as clean as if it had been scoured I liked to slide my hand along his warm back, threading my fingers among the curls of his conker brown coat as I watched for the moment when I must rescue the pail before he started bunting at it with all the bony-headed strength he would have bunted at his mother's udder.

When he was three months old Morag had warned me

that I must have him 'cut'. It was an offence to keep an uncastrated bull beyond a certain age and in Bruach the time for 'cutting' was in the spring 'before the flies came', Morag explained.

'What have the flies to do with it?' I asked in my ignorance.

'Ach, flies would likely get at the wound the same as they do with the sheep,' she told me. 'An' if the beast gets struck with the maggot the Dear knows but you could lose him altogether just.'

I shuddered at the idea of Sucky being 'struck with the maggot' and resolved to get the operation over as soon as possible. 'I suppose I'd better get in touch with the vet,' I said.

'Indeed no, mo ghaoil!' she protested. 'Why would you be wastin' money on a vet when Donald Beag will do it the same as he does for everyone else.'

In Bruach there were certain tasks which were always entrusted to certain men though whether this was because of aptitude or because their fathers had always done it before them or simply because they were self-appointed I do not know, but the fact that they were the only men who would be called upon to perform those tasks when necessary conferred on them a certain status. Erchy, though he grumbled about having to dig graves, was secretly proud of being the village gravedigger; Murdoch would have been hurt if it had been suggested that anyone but himself be called in to dose a sick animal and similarly Donald Beag would have been outraged if there had been the slightest hint that someone else could have attended to the castrating of a calf. He was proud of his job, so much so that when his own teeth had decayed so badly that he needed false ones he had been very particular that the dentist must understand how necessary it was for him to have perfectly fitting teeth so that he could continue as the village bull cutter.

It was Erchy who made the arrangements with Donald since no Bruach man would have dreamed of discussing such a subject with an Englishwoman and it was Erchy who arranged for Tearlaich and Padruig to come and help hold down Sucky while the operation was being performed. Donald had insisted that I must not be present in case I should 'put him off his aim' but when he arrived on the fateful morning and I pleaded with him to allow me to watch from behind a cow stall he agreed though he stipulated he must not be able to see or hear me.

'Have you got some Tarrapin Balsam?' he checked with me. I had been advised when I had first taken over my croft always to have a bottle of Terrebene Balsam handy, the Bruachites firmly believing that if their own skill coupled with a dose of 'Tarrapin' couldn't cure a sick animal then it wasn't worth calling the vet because the animal was doomed to die anyway. They used the balsam externally; they administered it internally; they even rubbed it on their own bodies when they had coughs or aches and pains and swore by its efficiency. I produced the bottle of balsam and handing it to Erchy led the way to the byre. Tearlaich who was the strongest of the four men threw Sucky on his side simply by pulling one of the calf's forelegs from under him. Padruig grasped one hind leg, Erchy the other and Tearlaich held the head, effectively quelling Sucky's struggles. In response to an annihiliating glower from Donald I dodged behind Bonny's stall and watched furtively as he took out his large clasp knife, wiped it clean on the leg of his far from

sterile looking homespun trousers and took Sucky's
testicles firmly in his left hand. With the knife he made a
small cut, then bending over and putting his mouth
to the cut he sucked gently and then bit. A moment later
he lifted his head and, turning, spat something out. He
bent and again sucked, then bit and spat; I glimpsed two
pink round shapes lying on the straw beside him. With a
satisfied grunt he reached for the bottle of balsam and
dabbed it liberally on the open wound. Then he stood up,
wiped his knife on his trousers, folded it and put it back
in his pocket. The three men also stood up releasing their
hold on Sucky who scrambled to his feet. He had made
no murmur of protest during the operation and now,
though he looked sulky and dishevelled, he did not appear
to be affected by his experience. I scratched his head
between the budding horns and offered him solace for his
lost virility in the shape of a potach before I followed the
men outside where I was in time to see Donald throw
something on to the manure heap beside the byre. Erchy
immediately grabbed a fork and threw a forkful of
bedding over it.

There was no payment for the bull cutting save the
requisite dram and for this we repaired to the kitchen.

'You have the makings of a fine beast there,' Donald
complimented me. 'You surely must have done him
well.'

'Too well,' grumbled Tearlaich, who was not noted
for rearing sturdy calves. 'There's no call for doin' a beast
as well as that.' He turned to me. 'You'll be after wishin'
you'd not fed him so well when he gets that big an' strong
you'll never manage to get a rope on him when it comes
to the time of the sale.'

As soon as he was old enough I put Sucky out on the

hill where he could mix with other stirks of his own age and like them fend for himself except for a daily bundle of hay during the winter. At least that was my intention but when the weather became really severe Sucky, who recognized his affinity with Bonny, tended to join her entourage and was quick to notice that whereas he was left out on the hill at night she was being brought home to a warm byre. He started to protest, following us right up to the moor gate and when I shut him out he would stand there looking at me through his fringe of hair and sounding so forsaken that after three nights I could withstand his pleading no longer and allowed him to come into the byre.

'You're surely no takin' in a grown stirk an' feedin' him,' scoffed my neighbours and when I merely smiled they warned, 'Ach, but you'll make him soft. A beast like that has all he needs on the hill an' he has a good coat to keep him warm.'

Sucky certainly had a splendid coat. The conker brown colour had lightened to that of milky tea; the tight curls had grown into long hair which the frequent rain shampooed to softness and the gales combed into sleek strands. As my neighbours claimed he was well equipped by nature to be outwintered on the hill but Bonny was so pleased to have his company and I got so much pleasure out of hearing two mouths munching at their hay that I slept more contentedly myself for his being inside. The only drawback was that there was twice as much dung to clean out in the morning.

'You should have sold that beast at the autumn sale,' Erchy told me. 'There's no sense in keepin' him eatin' his head off all winter.' But I had plenty of hay that year and despite his now ferocious appearance Sucky was such a gentle happy beast that I put off the moment of parting with him.

'I'll sell him in the spring,' I said and thought I meant it but when the spring came it was reported that prices at the sales were poor and I lunged at the excuse to keep him until the following autumn. Much as I hated the idea of parting with him I knew he had to go. He was now over eighteen months old, well grown and powerful, and even had the souming of my croft permitted it, which it did not, I could no longer keep a bullock which was just growing bigger and stronger and, I had to face it, tougher. There was no reprieve for him this time. Sucky had to go. And now on the day before the November sale I, like the other crofters who were selling their animals, had brought Sucky home from the hill. Unlike the other crofters however I had not needed to get helpers to round him up and corner him so that I could get a rope on him, for though he too had been made suspicious and apprehensive by all the chasing and shouting of humans and the wielding of sticks that was going on around him as the crofters separated their own beasts from the herd, he had come trustingly to me when I called; had stood quietly while I slipped the rope on his horns and had walked docilely beside me back to the croft. As he dove his head into a manger of sweet hay I tried not to think that this was probably the last time he would know such luxury.

I set the alarm for three o'clock the next morning and going out to the byre gave Sucky a final feed of hay. When I had eaten my own breakfast I returned to the byre and slid the rope once again round his horns. He was lying down and at first resisted my urging him to rise and when he eventually rose he had no wish to go out into the chill dark of the morning but I tempted him with a potach I

was taking to give him at the sale field and he began to
come unwillingly but without coercion. Once he had
winded the cattle already assembled at the gate of the
village, however, he became eager and I no longer had
to drive but merely to follow in his wake.

The night was still and cold, lit only by a few stars and
as I approached people called out interrogatively and we
exchanged greetings identifying one another by voice.
'It's time we were away,' someone said at last and as the
gate opened the restless snorting cattle, goaded by abuse
and sticks, burst through. We raced after them, keeping
them to the road; preventing them from scattering and
whipping up the more reluctant animals. It took an hour
before all the cattle had accepted the situation and
ceased their attempts to charge their way past us and back
to the familiarity of Bruach but then they settled down;
their pace slowed; the voices of the men dropped to con-
versational level, and I allowed myself to lag behind and
think of all that might be happening among the secret
wildness of the moors and hills around us and listening to
the noises of the droving: the small light hooves of the
young calves; the firmer hooves of stirks and the slow
plodding of old cows combining to form a percussion
chorus that was interspersed with the thud of a horn into
a cow's belly; the accompanying grunt of pain; the
clashing of two pairs of horns as animals disputed over
precedence; the shouts and thwacks of sticks as the men
rushed in to separate the combatants.

We had covered more than half the distance before a
slow dawn came sliding over the road, over the cattle and
over us and as we humans looked at each other, literally
in a new light, it seemed to me that we were all afflicted
with a momentary trace of shyness. The sun appeared

briefly, a half orb of fiery red above the mainland hills, but was engulfed so quickly by turgid dark clouds that it was as if a furnace door had been opened and then slammed shut. A chill breeze began to stir the pewter-grey water of the loch. With the increasing light the cattle seemed eager to increase their speed so that the drovers had similarly to increase their own pace to keep up with them. There was a mêlée of sorts when one of the more recalcitrant cows refused to cross a wooden bridge and turned in fright, charging the cattle and the drovers who thwarted her retreat and threatening to scatter the whole herd. The men tried beating her into submission but she dodged and charged until, realizing they would not give way, she jumped into the river and half-waded, half-swam across to the other side.

At the sale field over a hundred cattle were mustered and as I gave Sucky his last potach, his last scratch between the now formidable horns, before he went into the ring I compared him with the other beasts. There was no doubt he was a splendid animal and I had to admit to myself that I was exceedingly proud of having reared him. The bidding was brisk and when the sale was over and I had collected the bundle of notes from the auctioneer's clerk I had the satisfaction of knowing that Sucky had made the highest price of all the beasts at the sale.

'Aye, you had a good beast there right enough,' my Bruach friends told me, 'an' you ought to be feelin' well pleased with what you got for him.'

I was feeling well pleased but I was also feeling bereft. I ought never to have come, I told myself. I ought to have stayed at home and let Erchy dispose of Sucky as he had offered to do. Not wishing to stay to watch the animals being driven away by their new owners I started to walk back to Bruach. The men were all going on to the bar to spend some of their cattle money and if they were sober enough would be catching the bus back to Bruach later in the evening, but the Nurse, when she had heard I was attending the sale, had told me that she would be coming back that way round about mid-day so that if I started to walk she would pick me up along the road. I was sitting down eating my sandwiches when I saw her car.

'Did you enjoy the sale?' she enquired.

'I don't think "enjoy" is quite the right word,' I demurred.

'Were you pleased with the price you got?' she pursued.

'He made the best price at the sale,' I told her and I could not keep the pride out of my voice.

'If you were a man now you would be off celebratin' your success with a good dram as I daresay they are doing now,' she said with a sour twist to her mouth. I acknowledged her remark with a wan smile, not bothering to tell her that I felt more dejected than elated by my success.

That evening when I went to get Bonny there was a snowy howl to the rising wind and menace in the thick clouds that cushioned the black shapes of the hills. We were in for snow and I found myself hoping that Sucky was in a sheltered place and that he was not feeling too deserted. I hoped too that the calf Bonny was now carrying would not be another bull. It was too harsh an experience to rear a calf with pride as I had done and then dispose of it as I had disposed of Sucky. As I settled down to my evening meal I came to the depressing conclusion that I was not cut out to be either a crofter or a farmer and that the only way I wanted to work with animals was to conserve them. And then common sense crept in reminding me that to conserve one frequently has to cull. I went to bed early, worn out by my long demanding day. I would feel better about things in the morning, I told myself. Sleep and the congratulations of my neighbours would surely do much to restore my pride in my achievement. I put out the lamp and the darkness brought tears pricking at the back of my eyes. I turned my face into the pillow knowing that I had betrayed Sucky.

# The Stag

The stalker leaned on the gate at the entrance to his cottage, his telescope trained on the straggling party of sportsmen, ghillies and ponies wending its way down from the hills and silently he cursed the broken leg which had prevented him not only from being a member of the party but from being its accepted leader. The stalker was a man of the hills, exulting in their immensity and their brooding silence; their secret corries and clefts; their soaring ridges and sheer precipes and being a good stalker he revelled in his job. He continued to watch as the party trailed through the hollows of the glen, lowering his telescope only when the laird and his companions gained the road which led past the cottage.

'Well, MacDonald!' the laird hailed him as he approached. 'It's a great pity you couldn't have been with us. We had a damn good day. Two royals!' His face was red with exertion; his English accents sounded as if they were seeping through a port-soaked sponge.

'Indeed I'm pleased to hear that, my lord,' returned the stalker with a spectral gesture in the region of his deerstalker. 'And there is no one more sorry than myself that I was not able to be with you.' He tapped his plastered leg with his stick. 'He will not be so long before he is right again so the doctor is after telling me the day just.'

'Good, oh, very good!' responded the laird with awkward sympathy. 'We'll expect to see you back on the hill again quite soon then?'

'Not soon enough for me, my lord,' replied the stalker. The laird turned and nodded in the direction of a pony which, with a ghillie in charge, was plodding towards them, the carcass of a stag slung over its back. 'One of those brutes we got today was a real Methuselah,' he said. 'Should have been culled years ago I'd say. Hardly worth bringing home except for the antlers – and the hounds of course,' he added. The stalker was conscious of the hint of criticism in the laird's voice.

'Indeed then you must have got the wise old one that was away and over the hill to your neighbour's land whenever I've gone out after him,' he explained. 'Ach, he's the wily one, that one.'

The laird permitted himself a quick caw of laughter. 'Well, wily or not he's dead now,' he said. 'Very dead,' he repeated. He called some instruction to the ghillie then followed his companions in the direction of the shooting lodge.

The stalker waited until the pony drew level with the cottage. 'I hear you got good sport the day,' he greeted the ghillie. The ghillie halted the pony.

'No bad,' he replied. 'As much as will give the Englishmen a good appetite for their dinner tonight.' The stalker hobbled forward on his stick and inspected the dead stag. 'There's a good age on this beast,' observed the ghillie and his voice too was faintly critical.

'Aye, aye,' agreed the stalker. 'He has a good age on him right enough.'

It was ten years since he had stood as close as he was standing now to this particular stag. It had been an October day of sparkling sunshine that was bleaching the snowy peaks of the hills to a blue tinged whiteness and lighting the autumn sedge to a tawny gold. The wind was subtle and peat-scented; the boggy pools lay unruffled, screened by their palisades of rusty reeds, and when the stalker who had been trudging the hills since dawn had sat down at mid-day to eat his potach and to fortify himself from his hip flask he had reflected on his good fortune in having a job that needed only the qualifications with which he liked to think he was well endowed: health and strength; endurance; agility; a keenly observant eye and good marksmanship with a rifle.

When he had eaten and drunk he rested his back against a sun-warmed crag and stared up at the sky following the antics of a buzzard which was planing and circling over the corrie. At that time he had been courting Jeannie and as a consequence of her enthusiasm for dancing until the early hours of the morning the stalker had had three successive nights with only a snatched hour or two of sleep. He allowed himself to doze in the sunshine. When he woke it was to see that the sun was already spreading a golden fan over the horizon and he jumped up quickly remembering with dismay that he had promised Jeannie faithfully he would take her to a cinema that evening. It was to be the last showing of a film she particularly wanted to see and since the cinema was in the town and their only transport was by train the stalker knew his one chance of reaching his cottage in time to change and cycle the three miles to the station was not by tramping all the way round the loch and then climbing the hill but by taking a short cut along a narrow path that curved round the shoulder of the hill. Slinging his telescope round his neck and his rifle over his shoulder he strode forward urgently. It would not do to disappoint Jeannie; she was already peeved by the long hours he sometimes worked and there were too many other men who would quickly step into his place if it were vacant. He knew in his heart that she was not cut out to be the wife of a stalker; of a man so dedicated to the hills. He was aware that the town or its vicinity was the focus of Jeannie's ambition and yet, despite his knowledge he had to admit that he had allowed himself to fall deeply in love with her.

In half an hour he had reached the shoulder of the hill and pushing his forked stick into the ground to be collected another day he prudently unloaded his rifle. The path that lay before him was a dangerous one since

for about fifty feet of its length it was no more than a
ledge of rock, the width of three handspans, jutting out
from the slab sides of the hill like the tip of a tongue
caught between the teeth and with a sheer drop of some
hundred feet to a chaos of rocks below. But the stalker was
sure footed and since he had used the path once or twice
before it was with heightened alertness rather than
apprehension that he began cautiously on the traverse.
Turning his back to the drop and hugging the face of the
cliff with his body he sidled along concentrating on
ensuring that his thick-soled boots were firm on the ledge.
He had got about half way and was approaching the
section of the path which looped round a projection of
rock when he was startled to catch the rank scent of deer.
Turning his head he found himself confronted by the
stag. Instantly the stalker froze, realizing his peril. There
is no animal more aggressive than a rutting stag; nothing
it hates and fears more than the scent of a human and as
he saw the bristling mane, the lowered head and the ugly
menace in its eyes the stalker knew that neither he nor the
animal stood a chance of surviving the encounter. They
were both trapped: the stalker because if he attempted to
retreat the stag would immediately charge and inevitably
they would both plunge over the precipice to their deaths
on the rocks below: the stag was trapped because it could
neither back nor turn in the narrow sinuousness of the
path. He stared unblinkingly at the stag, subconsciously
noting the unusual pattern of the grey mottling on the
animal's left foreleg while he let himself realize that if the
stag charged it stood a faint chance of escaping with its
life: for himself there was no chance. His thoughts raced
through his mind like film through a speeded-up pro-
jector. Why was the stag here at all? he asked himself. In

all his years on the hill he had never known this particular
route to be used by deer. Why then had the stag chosen
to use it today of all days? For that matter why was he
here himself? The irony of the explanation smote him.
They were here because they were both victims of their
own desire: he was in a hurry to go to Jeannie; the stag
was in a hurry to go to a particular hind. It was as basic
as that! The stalker remained completely rigid. He had
no desire in him now except to live and as he held the
animal with his gaze he considered the possibility of using
his rifle. But it was slung over his left shoulder and he had
unloaded it before commencing the traverse. In his mind
he rehearsed the separate actions of inching the gun over
to his right; of extracting a cartridge from his pocket; of
loading the rifle. But he discarded the idea as being too
dangerously provocative to attempt. Even if he could get
hold of the rifle without movement that was perceptible
to the stag the click of opening and loading it would
assuredly send the beast crazy enough to spring to the
attack. As the man and the animal continued to assess
each other the stalker wondered if the stag was too
blinded by anger and ruttishness to be aware of its own
danger and as he glimpsed the setting sun reflected in
the animal's eyes, making them look even more malevo-
lent, he wondered how long it would wait before making
up its mind to take the risk and charge. He almost
hoped it would be soon for though the stag could doubt-
less remain in its position throughout the night he
knew that he could not. Even if he could the situation
would still be the same in the morning and since
he had always been a law unto himself so far as
hours were concerned he doubted if he would be
missed for a day or two so there was no likelihood of a

search party coming to his rescue. How long they stood facing each other the stalker did not know but suddenly he was aware that his knees, reacting at too long a spell of tautness, had begun to tremble. In that moment he made his decision. Slowly, so as not to excite the stag, he let his knees bend and then sag; let his arms droop fraction by fraction until they were on the ground behind him steadying him in a half crouching half reclining position. Instinct told him he must lie down and yet instinct also warned him that he must make no forward movement that might be interpreted by the stag as the beginning of a challenge. Gradually as his nerves and sinews would permit he eased himself backwards still holding the stag with his eyes. He saw the animal paw the path, the preliminary to combat; he felt the hard firm rock under his shoulders; he relaxed the muscles of his neck and pressing his side close against the face of the cliff he stretched himself out, flat on his back, submissive as a vanquished animal, one hand hanging over the precipice holding the empty rifle, his other hand across his crutch. The stalker closed his eyes and waited. There was a faint chance that this way the stag would accept his submission and being thus prevented from going forward would try to turn and in turning it would certainly fall, leaving the path clear for himself. But his heart began to pound and his body went rigid with panic as the smell of the stag grew stronger in his nostrils. The beast was coming on! He peered through half-closed eyelids and saw the stag's antlers silhouetted against the light; heard its hooves on the path. He closed his eyes again as he wondered how swift his death would be either by disembowelling or by being smashed on the rocks below. He felt a hesitant hoof on his thigh and the next moment the stalker grunted with pain as the weighted hoof coming down between his legs caught a fold of flesh on the inside of his leg, pinning it to the ground. He had time to brace every muscle in his body before the second hoof was planted firmly on his chest, squeezing the breath out of him with its weight. For one brief second he felt the stag's breath drift over his face and opening his eyes glimpsed the sky through the tracery of its antlers directly above him. The weight lifted from his chest to be immediately replaced by the weight of a hind hoof and almost before he could appreciate what was happening the stalker saw and smelled the semen-sticky underbelly of the stag as it shut out the sky for the fleeting seconds it took for the animal to pass over him. As he lay gasping he heard the sound of retreating hooves.

The stalker gulped the breath back into his lungs and rested his shaking limbs, too overwhelmed by the miracle of his escape to notice his pain and when the strength had flowed back into his body he got up and continued to sidle his way steadily along. Safely at the end of the path he sat down and drained his whisky flask while he reflected on the incredible uniqueness of his experience and vividly recalled the memory of the stag's antlers against the background of sky and its breath blowing over his face.

He was too late to keep his promise to Jeannie and when he met her the next day to apologize for his neglect he found himself reluctant to explain the reason for it suspecting her disbelief would make her still more peevish in her attitude towards him. He told no one in fact. Not even the pretty nurse who dressed the contusions on his chest and thighs and who later supplanted Jeannie in his affections to eventually become his wife. But subsequently he had kept a keen eye on the wanderings of the grey stag as he now called him, associating the animal in his mind with a hint of feyness and always when the laird was about to embark on a shoot the stalker, on the pretext of ensuring good sport, would go out the day before to locate the stag and send him with a few judiciously aimed shots bounding over the hill into the far corries which he knew none of the laird's companions would have the stamina to reach. And so the grey stag had continued unmolested. Even when it had grown old and had in its turn been bested in fight by younger and stronger stags he could not bring himself to cull it but had left it to roam the hills in peace, sometimes with a hind or two as its companions, sometimes solitary.

'Queer markings there on the leg,' remarked the ghillie, seeing the stalker's interest.

'Aye,' agreed the stalker, inspecting the mottled grey foreleg. The ghillie slapped the pony.

'I'd best be on my way if I'm to flesh this carcass tonight yet,' he said.

'Aye, you'd best do that,' the stalker told him. He hobbled back to the gate of the cottage and stood watching the pony plod on with its flopping burden.

He was glad he had not been at the killing.

# Winter Stack

'You have a good dung heap there,' observed Tearlaich thoughtfully. I acknowledged his remark with a smug smile. Having by this time acquired the crofter's and indeed the true farmer's attitude of near reverence to manure I was very proud of my large dung heap. I didn't know quite what I was going to do with it all but I was still very proud of it since theoretically the more muck one had the more crops one could grow. Being on my own with only a couple of animals and a few hens to provide for there was no need for me to grow large crops of anything; nor could I have harvested or stored or even sold them had I grown them and it might therefore have seemed the proportions of my muck heap were yet another instance of my growing Bruach acquisitiveness but since the cow byre had to be cleaned out regularly there was nothing else to do with the muck but to build it into a bigger and bigger heap and then in the spring spread as much as one's stamina would allow one to spread on the land. In Bruach the regularity of cleaning out the byre varied according to one's attitude to the task. Because I liked it less than most of the other croft work and because I found it less strenuous to take out a few forkfuls at a time I cleaned out my byre daily. Others preferred to clean theirs weekly. A few made the job an annual one, arguing that since a good layer of muck generated heat the cattle were warmer in the byre and thus needed less feeding while the vet had once told me of an old crofter who hadn't cleaned out his byre in fourteen years and when the vet went to attend his sick cow he had to climb up over a four-foot layer of dung to reach the animal.

When the spring came and it was time for the dung to be spread the crofters usually carried it in full creels on their backs, tipping out the manure by bending forward and letting it spill out over their heads. I knew that if I tried their method I should certainly have manure in my hair and ears and at least half way down my back so I preferred the wheelbarrow. I had been forking manure into the barrow when Tearlaich passed by.

'You'll never use all that,' he told me.

'No,' I said, shaking my head. 'I haven't the energy to get all that lot out anyway. It's heavy work.'

'Indeed an' don't I know that myself,' agreed Tearlaich. 'I believe the creel is a lot easier on you than the barrow all the same.'

'Maybe it is,' I said. 'But I still prefer the wheelbarrow.'

'Right enough,' he rejoined. 'A load of shit on your back can get pretty hot, I'm tellin' you. Even feelin' it through your clothes makes you sweat.' He watched me load until the barrow was as full as I could manage.

'I believe Ian over yonder would take a load from you if you've a mind,' he suggested. 'It would likely be worth a pound to him.'

'Really?' The idea of actually selling one of the by-products of my croft was, I thought, a step in the right direction but the idea of anyone actually wanting to buy manure struck me as strange: to come all the way from the next village to buy it sounded a little crazy. I wondered if Tearlaich was pulling my leg. 'Will I tell him when I see him?' he asked seriously.

'Oh, yes,' I replied, going along with him. 'If he likes to come for it he's welcome to a load.' I looked at him quizzically. 'Has he a big croft that he needs extra manure?' I enquired.

'Aye, he has three or maybe four crofts an' a good few beasts but he outwinters them mostly so he doesn't get the dung from them.' He slanted a smile at me. 'He's one of yon red-headed fellows they was speakin' of at the ceilidh the other night, you mind?'

'Oh, one of them!' I exclaimed.

'Aye,' responded Tearlaich. 'It was Ian's father, Red Alistair, that had the three red-headed sons an' when a

black-haired one came along he wouldn't believe the
babby was his. He wanted rid of it but then the mother
turned round an' told him the black-haired one was the
only one he had fathered anyway.'

'She must have had a penchant for red-headed men,'
I murmured.

'Ach, as I mind it she didn't much care about the
colour of their hair,' commented Tearlaich knowledgeably.

'What happened eventually? Did he get a divorce?'

'How would he do that when he'd never married her
in the first place?' asked Tearlaich reasonably.

It was nearer autumn than spring when a red-haired
man who already smelled strongly of dung turned up at
my croft along with a horse and cart and reminded me
that I had sent a message through Tearlaich back in the
spring that he could get from me a load of 'manyer'. I
showed him the heap and when he had finished loading
he came to the house and offered me a pound note that
was so caked with dung it looked like used toilet paper.
My reaction to dung fluctuated according to the seasons.
In winter when I myself was literally wading in it as I
cleaned out the byre and in spring when the whole
village reeked with the spread dung the sight and the
smell of it did not revolt me but in summer and autumn
because dung was 'entirely out of season', the cattle being
on the hill and the land having absorbed its mulch, I
found myself recoiling if I so much as trod on an old
cowpat. I overcame my slight reluctance to take the note
in my hand, recalling how old Murdoch had washed his
pound notes and hung them to dry on the clothes line
after a low-flying gull had 'spilled' on them and I decided
that I could follow his example.

'You still have plenty dung,' the red-haired Ian remarked enviously as he sat down to take the 'strupak' Highland hospitality demanded I give him. 'You must be wantin' to plant plenty potatoes come the spring.' His voice came out in blobs like thick sauce from a bottle and his blue eyes regarded me with only a glint of laughter. Morag, entering the room at that moment, heard his remark. 'Ach, Miss Peckwitt's after wantin' to grow all her food for herself. I believe she has a fancy for livin' by herself on one of the un-rabbited islands out there.'

'Is that so?' enquired Ian.

'I wouldn't mind trying it some day,' I told him, half seriously.

'Indeed you might just as well be in your grave as on one of them places,' he assured me. 'It's no place for a man to be on his own, never mind a lady,' he went on.

'Isn't that what I'm after tellin' her just,' exclaimed Morag, and Ian, seeing from my expression that I remained unconvinced, continued. 'An' what if you get sick there? I'm tellin' you,' he warned, 'in them places if whisky won't cure you then you have to die just for there's no help any place.'

I laughed. 'That settles it,' I told him. 'I'd welcome the one no more than the other.'

He turned an incredulous glance on Morag who nodded sad confirmation of my heresy and quickly changed the subject by asking after his wife.

'It's fine,' he replied. 'It's away to Glasgow next week to see its cousin.' I glanced at him in surprise. The Gaelic has no neuter and 'it' was seldom used by the Bruachites even when speaking English. I wondered where Ian had acquired the habit. He rose. 'Aye, well, I'd best be away. She'll be tired of waitin', likely.'

When he had gone I looked questioningly at Morag. 'Does he usually refer to his wife as "It",' I asked.

'I don't believe I've heard him ever call her anythin' but that,' she replied. 'An' I'm tellin' you, mo ghaoil, I doubt it's no so bad as some of the names he heard his own father call his mother.'

'Well, he did remember she was a "she": when he said she would be tired of waiting for him,' I reminded her.

'Indeed no, mo ghaoil,' she was quick to tell me. 'That was his horse he was speakin' of.' She picked up a magazine and flicked through its pages, asking would she 'get a read of it' when I had finished with it. I promised her she would. Then she said, 'What I came for rightly was to know when Erchy is to build your winter cock for you.'

'Tomorrow,' I replied. 'At least he said he'd come tomorrow if the weather holds but knowing Erchy. . . .' My voice trailed off and I shrugged my shoulders.

'If he comes then myself will give you a hand if the Lord spares me,' she vowed. 'That way we might get her finished before the rain is on again.'

Although it was now October my hay was not yet stacked for the winter but still stood in cocks ready, when the weather was fine enough, to be opened up, shaken out and built into the big stack from which every day throughout the winter I would pull the hay in handfuls until I had sufficient to fill a sack. A winter stack needed to be as sturdy as a house and the prerequisite for that was a skilful builder plus at least one other helper to throw up the hay. In the shortening autumn days it was almost imperative to have yet another helper to spread the hay so as to give it its final airing before it was packed into what Morag called 'the winter cock' and I was

indeed grateful for her offer of help. That night when I
returned from shutting up the hen house the land and the
sea were quiet and still and I looked anxiously out across
the bay where a trace of orange sunset lingered pinched
between the horizon and a sky which was already studded
with frost-kindled stars. It looked to me as if the weather
would hold for tomorrow and I prayed that Erchy would
keep his promise. The building of winter stacks of hay
and corn was very nearly the climax of the year's toil.
Only the clamping of the potatoes and the salting of the
herring remained to be done before the winter closed in
and I was eager to see my hay secured. I grew only a
small amount of corn and between us Morag and I had
managed to build the corn stack, but the hay was not
only more abundant, it was more necessary. Corn was only
a supplement and one's cattle could survive without it;
they would be unlikely to survive without hay.

The morning dawned calm and cold but by ten o'clock
a light frost which had brushed the grass was dispersed
by mellow sunlight that poured over the crofts like melted
butter. At eleven o'clock which, Erchy maintained,
because of the dew was the earliest it was safe to start
work, he arrived and after quickly estimating the quantity
of hay he began to prepare the base for the stack using
for this the damp caps of dry grass which Morag and I
had already lifted from the cocks. The base is of para-
mount importance since it predetermines the shape of the
finished stack. If the diameter is too wide for the amount
of hay to be built upon it then it will be too squat to shed
the rain; if it is too narrow it will be high and unstable.
Once he was satisfied with the proportions of the base
Erchy climbed on to it and standing in the centre called:
'Ready now!' The real work began. Working round and

round the stack Morag threw him forkfuls of hay which he spread and continuously trod down while I brought up supplies of hay from the surrounding cocks, fluffing it up in a circle round the stack not only so that it would sweeten in the sunshine but because I had been warned that it was essential no lumps of hay should be built into the stack.

There is something deeply satisfying about working in the hay particularly when it is wild, leafy, sweet smelling hay such as we made in Bruach and my satisfaction was enhanced by the fact that I was working to the accompaniment of rippling Gaelic voices backed by the trilling of the sea; the excited cries of gulls proclaiming their discovery of autumn herring; the barking of rutting stags echoing from the hills; the investigative 'tlonks' of ravens and the delighted mewing of buzzards as both young and adult birds soared and planed in celebration of their autumn reunion. It seemed to me that there was joy all around us; on the land, on the sea and in the air and though after hours of continuous work my arms and shoulders were aching and I felt that I was labouring in a stupour of raking and shaking and forking I knew myself to be exquisitely content. Erchy's glossy red face rose above us as my stack climbed higher and higher and the number of small cocks diminished. It would not be long now, I was telling myself.

Morag said, 'I'm thinkin' the rain's no far away.' I turned to look at her askance as she dug her hayfork into the ground and held on to it with both hands as if for support while she scanned the sea.

'Oh, no!' I protested. Everything had been going so well that I had been too absorbed to perceive how the sun had paled at the approach of an army of dark clouds which were massing over the outer islands. Now as I paused I could see the treachery in the sky and feel the breeze renewing its strength.

'You'd best not open up any more of those cocks,' Erchy warned. 'We'll maybe have time to finish what we have spread just before she'll be here.' I felt myself sagging with tiredness. The stack was two-thirds built and if only the weather had lived up to its early morning promise I would have been able to go to bed blissful in the knowledge that my hay was secure for the winter. But when the rain came and there was no doubting now that it was being pushed closer and closer by the wind I would have to revert once more to staying constantly attuned to the portents of the sky; to trying to anticipate the attempts of the wind to destroy my haycocks and to trying to steal a march on the frequent squalls while I waited for the promise of another fine day which would coincide with Erchy's availability and inclination to complete the stack building. As the first splodgy raindrops fell coldly on our tingling arms and faces we pulled the tarpaulin over the top of the unfinished stack, weighted it down with boulders tied to the corners, and as I leaned my fork and rake against the wall of the barn I thought that even the prospect of a respite from work was little solace for my disappointment at not seeing the job completed. The rain brought an early twilight and we returned to the house for a meal of rabbit casserole which had been keeping warm in the oven. In the lamplight I saw that Morag's face looked drawn and tired and I was ashamed of having allowed her to work so hard. Physically her job had been the most demanding but both she and Erchy had insisted that it was she who must throw up the hay since on a croft even the most simple looking tasks required a degree of expertise and neither of them considered me skilful enough to do the job. 'Not without I'd be havin' to swear at you, an' I wouldn't want to do that,' Erchy explained.

'You'll have plenty hay this winter,' said Morag. 'Even supposin' you don't get any more of it into the stack you'll do well enough.'

'Unless she buys in another beast,' suggested Erchy. They looked at me as if expecting an answer.

'Yes, I have thought of that,' I admitted. There was a subsidy on cows and since my croft had yielded well I thought I might just as well draw two lots of subsidy as one. 'Have you heard of anyone who's thinking of selling a good cow?' I asked them.

'Ach, you shouldn't be thinkin' of buyin' in a cow,' Erchy told me. 'You'd be best to get a calf an' rear it yourself.'

'And where will I get a calf at this time of year?' I put to them. They shook their heads and murmured dubiously.

'It's a pity yon fellow they used to call the "black drover" isn't still alive,' said Erchy.

'Did he have good calves?' I asked.

'He'd give any woman that went to bed with him a good calf,' returned Erchy. 'An' they were the best, too. He'd make sure of that.'

'Whis!' Morag chided him. 'Miss Peckwitt doesn't want to be told things like that.'

'Why not?' demanded Erchy. 'He's dead now so she's too damty late anyway.'

'Ach, you're a terrible man for the lies,' she told him.

'It's no lie indeed,' began Erchy but Morag silenced him with an arrogantly lifted hand. I glimpsed the trace of a smile touching Erchy's mouth as he fixed his attention on a ceiling beam immediately above his head. We heard the drone of an engine which ceased outside the house.

'That's the nurse surely,' said Morag. In Bruach, except in summer when the tourists poured into the village, one could identify engine noises as being that of the bus, the grocery van or the nurse's car and since it was not time for the bus and not the right day of the week for the grocery van to come then it needed little reasoning to know that the only remaining probability was the nurse's car. A few moments later the nurse bounced into the kitchen. Unlike the Bruachites she, being no Highlander, professed always to be in a hurry.

'I mustn't stay,' she announced with practised breathlessness, 'but I just wanted to ask you if you're going to this dance Flora's on about. I said I'd find out for her how many were going and what I was thinking was if you'd like to go as a nurse you could borrow one of my uniforms.' Her eyes went wistfully to the table where there was a plate of small iced cakes and another of sliced bunloaf.

'Surely you have time to take a strupak,' I invited.

'It looks so tempting,' she confessed and promptly sat down beside Erchy. 'I'll just take a cup in my hand.'

Erchy pushed the plate of cakes towards her. 'Take one seein' this is what you came for anyway,' he teased. She blinked away a coy smile as she took a cake.

'What do you think about this dance?' she asked, looking at me.

'I'm not going,' I told her.

'You're not?' I shook my head. 'You used to enjoy a dance,' she reminded me.

'Ach, she's thinkin' she's too old for them now,' Erchy informed her and the nurse, who was some years older than I, blushed. He was right, of course. I was getting too old for such capers and Bruach dancing was so rigorous that at the end of each dance the partners did not thank each other politely but thanked God audibly.

'Oh, do come,' pressed the nurse. But I would not be persuaded.

'I never did like fancy dress dances anyway,' I added by way of excuse.

'What are you dressin' up as yourself?' Erchy asked her but she would not tell him. 'There's a good few goin' all the same,' he told her and nodded across at me. 'Yon man that was over here buyin' your dung was tellin' me he's thinkin' he might go himself.'

'What will be be after dressin' himself up as?' asked Morag.

'Indeed I don't know. Unless he's plannin' to go as a heap of manyer an' that's why he came to get the dung when he did.'

The nurse sniffed. 'He wouldn't need to dress up much if that's what he's going as,' she said with elegant sarcasm. She put down her cup. 'I must go anyway,' she told us. 'I have to see Alistair yet tonight.'

'I'll go with you, then,' Erchy proposed. 'I told the cailleach I'd go some time.'

Together they went out into the now wet and blustery evening and through the window we saw the headlights of the car probing their way along the narrow road. I had got out of the habit of drawing the curtains since in Bruach one did not want to shut out the night but rather to allow it to share one's company. Morag sighed. 'I'd best be away myself,' she said but I pressed her to stay and brewed another pot of tea and while we sat at the table drinking it she told me of her childhood; of sitting round the peat fire which was in the centre of the room;

of her mother and grandmother spinning and carding wool in the evenings; of herself knitting stockings for the family; of their unquestioning belief in curses and the powers of some people to lift them; of her own longing to go to school. 'Aye, an' I mind when I was at school first there was this new teacher came from the mainland an' he got us children singin',

> *"Jesus is my dearest friend,*
> *I love him more than coal."* '

'Coal?' I interrupted.

She nodded. 'That's what we used to sing right enough until one day he tells us to say the words just an' not sing them an' when he hears us say "coal", says he, "It's not coal, children, but gold", though he didn't think to tell us what gold was an' none of us cared to ask him. So we sang about gold an' I mind when we young ones got outside we were after askin' each other what like of stuff it was. See,' she explained, 'we'd none of us heard of it or seen the like of it that we knew of. We knew coal was kind of precious since it was only the laird that could afford to buy it so we knew we'd have to be lovin' Jesus plenty if we loved him more than coal but we didn't know what use there would be for this stuff called gold. We children made it up between us that it must be some sort of stuff that warmed you better than coal.' She looked at my astonished face. 'There now,' she said, 'that's how far back we were in those days.'

'When did you first see a coal fire,' I asked her.

'Not till I was workin' at the laird's house an' I was sixteen by then,' she replied. 'One of the things I had to do there was to get in the coal for the fires an' I mind thinkin' the first time I had to do with it that we children must have made Jesus awful sad to be singin' to him that we only loved him more than these pails of dirty black stuff I was after carryin'.' She smiled reminiscently. 'Aye, but those days are gone an' now there's not a one that cannot afford to buy coal to burn along with their peats, even if they don't see much gold.' The room was quiet except for the buffeting of the wind and the whine of a draught under the door.

'Was there much entertainment in those days for the young people?' I asked her.

'Indeed more than there is now,' she replied. 'There was shinty for the men an' then the laird would give a dance at the backend of the year for the estate workers an' anyone that had a mind to come. These days you'll not see a dance in Bruach from one year to the next.'

'Did you do much dancing?'

'When I was young I did,' she admitted.

'Did you ever fall in love?' I pursued.

Her mouth was softened by a fugutive smile. 'Not love the way you English would have it,' she told me. 'But I wasn't passed by,' she added proudly.

'No one special?' I persisted.

'Ach, there was a young gamekeeper at the time helpin' out the regular gamekeeper but he was such a dour one I didn't know for sure was he wantin' me or not.'

'How was he dour?'

'Ach, he was that feart of folks makin' a game of him, though why they would I don't know for he was a well set up young man. I mind him at the laird's dance one time an' I knew he was wantin' to catch my eye but I was thinkin' to myself that if he hadn't the nerve to ask me to dance then he wasn't the man for me anyway.'

157

'Did he ask you?'

'Aye, well, he works his way round to where I'm sittin' an' makin' out I'm not seein' him at all. Then when he's right beside me he says quietly, "Are ye dancin'?" No more than that just but "Are ye dancin'?". Says I without lookin' at him, "Are ye askin'?" Says he, "I'm askin'." Says I, "I'm dancin'," and with that we started dancin' together but he never spoke another word to me the rest of the night.'

'Did you meet him again?'

'Indeed I did so but seein' he was that slow makin' up his mind I thought I was best off without him though he was a fine young fellow. I couldn't have had him anyway for my parents needed the money I was gettin' workin' for the laird an' after about a year or two of courtin' me with his eyes just as you might say he was away to the mainland for another job an' I never heard of him again.' She sighed. 'Ach, I liked him well enough but he would never have done for my parents seein' he wasn't from these parts.' She yawned. 'It must be at the back of ten,' she said and looked at the clock, which said it was twenty past six. My clock almost always said it was twenty past six. It was a seven-day clock which had been given to me by an English friend who when she had stayed with me had been distressed because I rarely used clock time. Now that I had a clock I was not much better since I wound it only on impulse; just as I would decide to wash curtains or bake an angel cake, I would decide to wind the clock and since the impulse came only about four times a year for three hundred and thirty-seven days out of three hundred and sixty-five my clock gave the time as twenty past six. Morag rose and pulling her buttonless jacket over her chest she tied it with a belt of rope and refusing the offer of a hurricane lantern dove out into the night leaving me to muse over the image of the diffident young gamekeeper and his approach to the equally diffident young Morag.

'Are ye dancin'?'

'Are ye askin'?'

'I'm askin'.'

'I'm dancin'.'

It was such an illustrative example of tight-lipped Highland reserve that I went over it again and again until it had settled in my mind like a formula.

Two weeks were to pass before there dawned a morning that gave promise of a calm dry day suitable for stack building and, as luck would have it, on that day I had arranged to catch the bus to the mainland. Two friends of mine, Sue and her husband Robert, were coming to pay me a visit and I had promised to go over to the mainland to meet them and their car and guide them along the road to Bruach. As I waited on the pier for their arrival I looked at the serene blue sky and the lazy sea and as I felt the genial smile of the sun I thought if only I had been home in Bruach I could no doubt have persuaded Erchy to finish my winter stack for me. My visitors were delayed on their journey and it was nearly dusk when we reached Bruach and just as I had lit the lamp and was telling my guests to make themselves comfortable while I rushed round seeing to the outside chores Morag appeared in the doorway. I introduced her and suggested that she might like to stay for the strupak I would shortly be making but she resisted firmly. 'I have fed your hens,' she told me as she saw me start to prepare mash.

'Oh, bless you Morag, you're a treasure,' I told her. She made a deprecating gesture, then still standing in the open doorway she turned and pointed out into the gathering dusk and to my delight but to the utter bewilderment of my two guests she declared dramatically: ' 'Tis no myself would be botherin' Miss Peckwitt but 'tis Erchy that's wantin' her to go to him just so he can show her the beautiful shaped cock he has waitin' for her out there.'

## The Croft in Between

My friends, Robert and Sue, were so impressed by the slow pace and the contentment of life in the Highlands they became enamoured with the idea of looking for a place of their own. Bruach, they decided, was too wild and barren for them to think of settling even had there been a croft available.

'You ought to write a book and call it "How Bare was my Bruach"!' suggested Sue.

After much map searching and much scanning of the newspapers which circulated in the crofting counties they came to the conclusion that their best course was to make a leisurely tour of the Highlands and keep an eye open for a place which offered what they were seeking, i.e. tranquillity without isolation; beauty without barrenness. They suggested I accompany them and since Morag was there when the idea was first mooted she volunteered immediately to look after my cow and hens. There was little to do on the croft now that my winter stack was complete. Bonny was still out on the hill and needed only to be milked and given a bundle of hay each day. The hens had to be fed and the eggs collected but until Bonny had to be brought in to the byre at night I was relatively free and the temptation to accept the invitation and see parts of Scotland I had never previously visited was strong indeed.

'Of course she'll come,' Morag assured them with such emphasis that I think they expected me to begin packing right away.

We set off a few days later and in golden sunshine made for the remoter parts of the Highlands, spending the night wherever reasonably attractive lodging offered accommodation so late in the season when snow was already capping the sable hills and the yellow-reeded bogs and pools were stilled by frost. We had enjoyed Highland hospitality everywhere. The colder the night the warmer the fires they built for us; the more blankets they piled on our beds; the more hot water bottles they put in them; the more food they loaded on to our plates. 'Marvellous people,' Robert frequently observed.

'They all look so happy and serene,' said Sue. 'I've always thought Highlanders were dour and uncommunicative but it simply isn't true.'

It is really asking too much to make one's first tour of the Highlands and house-hunt at the same time. One becomes so overwhelmed by the vastness of one's surrounding; by the superabundance of hill peaks; the glory of lochs; the slightly intimidating desolation of the moors, that one is capable of doing little else but marvel at their wildness. So it was with Robert and Sue. Though they saw many deserted looking croft houses in situations which strongly appealed to them ferreting out information regarding their owners and the possibility of sale had proved, as I suspected it might, a frustrating task for a tourist. 'I have never before experienced such courteous dissimulation,' Robert complained. 'They seem willing to give one almost anything but the information one wants. I believe sometimes I'm actually talking to the owners of the place I'm enquiring about without them ever betraying the fact,' he ended with a chuckle.

'I think you might find it more rewarding to put an advertisement in one of the Highland papers,' I suggested meekly.

'I think you're possibly right,' Robert conceded and thereafter we gave only desultory attention to house hunting and simply allowed ourselves to revel in the scenery. We had enjoyed splendid weather for our trip; indeed Robert and Sue had not seen a drop of rain since they had set foot in Scotland but the day before we were due to return to Bruach there was a perceptible difference in the day.

'I shan't mind going back to the office nearly so much if the weather turns nasty before we leave,' Robert said.

'The office!' moaned Sue. 'After this.' We were having a picnic lunch on a hill overlooking a long narrow loch that was like a blue furrow between ridges of the hills and not even the croak of a hoody crow or the bleat of a sheep broke the all-enveloping silence. I understood the despair in her voice.

We returned to the car and it was as if we had absorbed some of the silence for none of us spoke until Robert brought the car to a stop outside a small hotel whose front lawn bordered the loch.

'This looks okay,' he said and went to enquire as to the possibility of our spending the night there. When he reappeared he was nodding affirmatively. As we took our overnight bags out of the car we felt the first sleety cold drops on our faces.

We were the only guests at the hotel and after eating a traditional and immensely satisfying high tea we were invited by the friendly old couple who apparently owned the hotel to forsake the indifferent comfort of the residents' lounge for the snugness of their private living room, one end of which was conveniently bounded by the back entrance to the bar. Robert suggested drinks but the old man held up his hand and a moment or two later his wife appeared with a tray on which there were five glasses of whisky and a jug of peat tinted water. We raised our glasses to the old couple and wishing them 'Slainte Mhath!' began sipping what was to me the mellowest whisky I have ever tasted in my life. The old man questioned us about our travels and in turn Robert plied him with enquiries about crofts that might be for sale but, as always, it seemed that the crofts in the vicinity were claimed by the locals or by their relatives who even though they might live on the mainland still held on to the houses as holiday homes or as places they hoped to retire to.

'Ach, but this is a gey lonely place,' said the old woman. 'I doubt you would want to live here.'

I looked at Sue. I had no doubt of her desire to live in the Highlands but I guessed she would soon be wanting more company and more amenities than a lonely croft could provide. But it was nice that she should have her dream.

The old man had a folded newspaper on his knee and I asked him if there was anything of interest in it. He offered it to me and pointing a finger to a headline said, 'I was just readin' to Peggy the piece about the twin brothers. Now that's a strange thing, do you not think so?' I began to read.

'Read it aloud,' pleaded Sue, so I read them the report of twin brothers, one of whom had been engaged to the daughter of the local gamekeeper, but a few weeks before the marriage was to take place he had been killed in an accident. Some time later the surviving twin had become engaged to the same girl but only forty-eight hours before the wedding day he too had met with a fatal accident. The gamekeeper's daughter was quoted as saying she 'had the feeling that her first fiancé had reached out beyond the grave and prevented the marriage'.

'Aye, that would be the way of it just,' said the old man. 'There's things happen in these parts that's so strange when you come to tell of them folks don't believe you.' He sat back in his chair and puffed at his pipe. 'And since no Highlander can bear to be thought a liar,' he went on, 'then they don't trouble themselves to tell of these things.' His bright blue eyes regarded us challengingly through a mist of tobacco smoke.

'Well that story of the twins certainly sounds a fascin-
ating coincidence,' said Sue, who shared my appetite for
'coincidences'.

'Aye, indeed but there's plenty says these things are
true enough,' maintained the old man.

'What things?' asked Robert, lifting his empty glass
and also his eyebrows to indicate that it was his turn to
stand a round. The old woman took our glasses and while
we waited for her to refill them only the snarl of the
flames round the logs on the fire and the sad keening of
the wind as if over the passing of autumn broke the
silence. The old woman placed our full glasses in front of
us and sat down again.

'It's true that the spirit can reach out beyond the
grave,' explained the old man in answer to Robert's
question. He took a good sip of his whisky and looked
across at his wife. She glanced up from her knitting and
I had the distinct impression she had given him a nod of
permission. 'There was the like of such a thing not so far
from here,' he continued. 'It was a good few years back
now but just the same I remember it well enough.' Sue
and I exchanged delighted smiles. We guessed there was
a story coming and neither of us could have chosen a
better way to spend the evening than by listening to a tale
beside a log fire in a lamplit room.

'There was these three crofts, see, at the head of the
loch,' went on the old man. 'An' they were owned by
three brothers. It was one big croft just when the father
was alive but in dyin' he split it among his three sons so
it wouldn't seem as if he was favouring the one more than
the other. But ach, it made the crofts that small and
awkward to work that two of the brothers agreed they
would work theirs together as well as they could which

was not all that easy seeing the third brother had the croft that lay in between their own crofts. I hardly like to say it but the third brother was always the jealous one; right from a youngster he was spiteful an' thrawn as they say; what we would call in the Gaelic a "Greannach".' He looked at me. 'You will have come across that word, I doubt?' he asked. I nodded. 'Aye well, the Greannach was that blinded by spite against the other two he would as often spoil himself in trying to prevent them making the best use of their crofts.' He looked at the bottom of his empty glass and gestured to us to finish ours. Sue and I refused firmly but the old woman filled the glasses for the two men. 'Ach, it was a foolish thing the father did, that, splitting up the croft though no doubt he was tellin' himself it was for the best.' He kicked back a log that had rolled out of the fire. 'An, the time goes on,' he resumed, 'an' the Greannach got himself a wife an' then they had a daughter. Then another brother married an' had a son. The other brother didn't marry at all so when he died he left his croft to the son of his brother so that after a time the son came to own two of the three crofts. What then could be better than that he should marry his cousin, the daughter of the Greannach, so the three crofts would be one again? The young man set about courting his cousin but though she herself was pleased enough to have him her father refused to let her. She was old enough by then to choose for herself but the Greannach was so determined the young man shouldn't have his croft that he threatened if his daughter married her cousin she should never inherit it. Ach, it was a pity an' more than a pity right enough for I believe the young man would have made his cousin a good husband an' the three crofts together would have given them as good a livin' as they needed for these

parts. But seein' her father was so set against it the girl
wouldn't go against him. No son or daughter of the croft
would want it to go to a stranger an' seein' there was no
other relations nearer than Australia strangers is what
they would have been, so the girl maybe acted wise
enough. Even on his deathbed the Greannach was after
makin' his daughter swear she wouldn't marry her cousin
an' what she said to quiet him no one but herself would
know but after he died she got the croft. A couple of years
went by an' the young man thought maybe it was time
he tried his luck with his cousin again. She didn't take
much persuadin' seein' she'd not been over fond of her
father with his mean ways an' his sharp temper an' since
she was thirty past an' a wee bitty deaf an' a wee bitty
short-sighted she knew well enough she'd not be likely to
get another chance if she waited. So they arranged the
weddin' an' the young man was well pleased at the
thought of the three crofts bein' one again an' he planned
how he'd work it the next season without being girned at
for lettin' his cow put a foot over the boundary or maybe
takin' a sweep of grass that wasn't his. The weddin' was
planned for November for then all the harvest would be
in but that summer an' autumn were so wet the work was
held up again an' again an' they had to delay the weddin'
until the New Year. Ach, it was terrible weather that
year; great pourings of rain that turned the crofts into
bogs that the cattle churned up with their hooves; the
drains overflowin' so there was that much mud goin' into
the wells you couldn't take a drink of water without lettin'
it settle in the pail for an hour or two after you'd taken it
from the well. An' the burns were that swollen they
flowed white like snow down the mountainside.' He
paused and stared meditatively into the fire; his wife

reached for a pair of spectacles and started to count the
stitches on her needles; Robert lit another cigar and Sue
and I sat quite still waiting for the old man to continue
his story.

'Three days before the weddin' the girl was thinkin' she
ought to go an' tidy up her father's grave seein' it was
comin' up to the New Year an' seein' she was goin' to
flout him anyway. She'd done him well, mind, an' had a
fine gravestone erected for him only six months before an'
had his name put on it along with the date of his death
an' a 'Rest in Peace' to calm him down as she thought,
but she was keen he should be spruced up for Hogmanay.
The burial ground was about three miles away round the
other side of the loch an' the rain was still pourin' down
when she left the house but ach, she didn't mind rain;
she was well used to it. It was after dark that evenin' when
the young man went to her house to do his bit of courtin'
an' when he found the place in darkness an' the peats
cold on the hearth he was askin' himself where she could
be. The cattle were still standin' beside the byre wantin'
in an' the henhouse wasn't closed up so he guessed the
hens hadn't been fed. He looked around the croft an'
shouted but gettin' no sight nor sound of his cousin he
made for the shepherd's house to ask did they see her anywhere. Right enough, they told him, she'd called there
on her way to the burial ground but they had no seen her
comin' back yet. The shepherd an' the young man
thought they'd best go lookin' for the girl an' they took
lanterns an' set out callin' out her name as they went
along. It was in the burial ground itself they found her an'
at first all they could make out was her boots stickin' out
from beneath the heavy gravestone. Seemingly the ground
had got that soft with all the rain an' the gravestone

hadn't been given a chance to settle properly an' it had toppled over an' crushed her just as she was leanin' over attendin' to the grave.' The old man drained his glass.

'She was dead?' whispered Sue.

'Oh, aye, right enough she was dead,' said the old man. 'It was a fine handsome tombstone she'd got for him an' there was a good weight in it.'

The old woman spoke. 'If that wasn't the spirit reachin' beyond the grave I don't know what is,' she said.

'It's uncanny,' breathed Sue. The old man nodded.

'So the young man didn't get the croft in between after all?' I commented.

'Aye, he got it all right,' replied the old man. We all looked at him enquiringly. 'Like I was sayin', there was no closer relations than the ones in Australia an' they weren't wantin' home to claim it so the young man applied to the Land Court that has to do with these things an' they agreed he should take it over. So he got the three crofts together again as they'd been in his grandfather's time an' he has them to this day.'

'Good,' I said. 'I hope he prospered.'

'He worked the three crofts together an' he married an' I'm thinkin' he prospered,' affirmed the old man.

'So the father's vengeance, if that's what it was, was wasted,' observed Robert.

'It was indeed,' replied the old man. 'But then did I not tell you the man was a Greannach that would as often spoil himself with his spitefulness?' He got up and rooting in a cupboard beside the fireplace produced a book from which he extracted a small newspaper cutting. The headline read, 'Father's Tombstone Kills Daughter' and below it, as if it had been a fairly unremarkable experience, it gave a few sketchy details of the incident along with the verdict that it had occurred because of the phenomenally wet weather. I handed the cutting back to the old man and he replaced it carefully between the pages of the book.

The next morning we bade the old couple goodbye and continued on our way. We had not gone far before we noticed an abandoned croft house quite close to the road and Sue insisted on getting out to take a closer look. 'I wonder who owns this one and if they would sell it?' she murmured.

'To us?' asked Robert facetiously.

'Why not?' she replied. 'Just think if we could have a cottage like this to come to in the summer. All this lovely remoteness and silence.'

'Not so remote from the hotel,' I pointed out, 'and I imagine there'll be plenty of tourists here in the summer.'

'But you can't see the hotel from here,' argued Sue. 'That's what matters.'

'Look, Sue,' Robert reminded her patiently. 'Even if we could buy it we would need to do it up before we could live in it and what time would we have to do it up? Holidays wouldn't be much fun if we had to spend them indoors working to make the place habitable.'

'You are so disgustingly practical,' Sue complained and with a shrug of her shoulders got back into the car. As we cruised along we saw another abandoned croft house and since it was not so derelict as the previous one Sue once again insisted on getting out to inspect it. 'I wish we could find out who owns these two empty places,' she said. 'This one wouldn't take much doing up before we could spend our holidays in it and then if we ever could escape permanently it would be a wonderful place to dream of coming to.'

We stood together admiring the situation. It certainly

was an attractive spot set among the snow shawled hills and looking out over the waters of the loch which this morning were racing before a pettish breeze. We heard a shout and turned to see a shepherd calling his dog to heel.

'Ask him,' urged Sue, prodding Robert's arm. We waited until the shepherd came abreast of us.

'It is a cold day,' he greeted us cordially. We agreed it was. 'I'm thinkin' the snow will be with us again soon enough,' he added.

'Go on!' hissed Sue.

'I wonder,' Robert began as the shepherd was about to walk away, 'can you tell us who owns this cottage and whether there's a chance of it being for sale?'

The shepherd came back to where we were standing beside the car. He was surprisingly forthcoming.

'It is owned by the man that has the hotel there,' he told us. 'Did you not spend the night there?' We told him we had. 'Ach, but I doubt he would be selling it. There's plenty of visitors been wantin' to get it from him in the summer.' I both saw and sensed Sue's disappointment.

'Well what about the one further back down the road,' she persisted. 'Who owns that one?'

'The one in between this an' the croft where the hotel now stands?' he asked. Sue nodded. 'That belongs to the old man too,' replied the shepherd, giving her a compassionate grin. 'But I'm thinkin' he's even less likely to sell that one. He had a job gettin' it an' he's not wantin' for money.' Sue made a disappointed grimace. 'Maybe you wouldn't want to be livin' in that house supposin' you could get it,' he told her, inclining his head in the direction of the first house we had seen. 'There's somethin' queer always about that place.'

'Queer?' echoed Sue. 'Do you mean haunted?'

'Indeed I don't know if it is haunted but it was never a happy house. It belonged to a young woman once that was going to marry someone her father had forbidden her to marry an' though she waited until he was dead before she fixed the weddin' she was killed three days before the day.'

'Her father's tombstone fell on her,' said Sue.

'Aye?' The shepherd was surprised. 'You will be knowin' the story then?'

'Yes, we know it,' Sue told him. 'Oh well, thanks for telling us,' she said. The shepherd continued on his way and we got back into the car.

'So it was the old man at the hotel who was once the young man who wanted the croft in between,' said Robert. We had rounded the loch now and were looking across to where the hotel stood close to the margin of the shore. To the right of it we could see the two abandoned croft houses set almost equidistant from each other.

'And the young man worked the three crofts and he married and he prospered,' Sue mimicked the old man's rich Highland accents.

'And why not?' Robert demanded. 'After all, he does serve damn good whisky.'